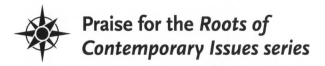

Praise for the *Roots of Contemporary Issues series*

"Everything around us—policy, population, culture, economy, environment—is a product of the actions and activities of people in the past. How can we hope to address the challenges we face and resolve contentious issues—like inequality, health, immigration, and climate change—without understanding where they come from? The volumes in the Roots of Contemporary Issues series are the tested products of years of classroom teaching and research. They address controversial issues with impartiality but not detachment, combining historical context and human agency to create accounts that are meaningful and usable for any student confronting the complex world in which they will live."

—TREVOR R. GETZ, *San Francisco State University*

"This is a truly innovative series that promises to revolutionize how world history is taught, freeing students and faculty alike from the 'tyranny of coverage' often embedded within civilizational paradigms, and facilitating sustained reflection on the roots of the most pressing issues in our contemporary world. Students' understanding of the importance of history and their interest in our discipline is sure to be heightened by these volumes that deeply contextualize and historicize current global problems."

—NICOLA FOOTE, *Arizona State University*

D0976300

ROOTS OF CONTEMPORARY ISSUES

RUPTURED LIVES

ROOTS OF CONTEMPORARY ISSUES

Series Editors

Jesse Spohnholz and Clif Stratton

The **Roots of Contemporary Issues** Series is built on the premise that students will be better at facing current and future challenges, no matter their major or career path, if they are capable of addressing controversial issues in mature, reasoned ways using evidence, critical thinking, and clear written and oral communication skills. To help students achieve these goals, each title in the Series argues that we need an understanding of the ways in which humans have been interconnected with places around the world for decades and even centuries.

Published

Ruptured Lives: Refugee Crises in Historical Perspective
Jesse Spohnholz, Washington State University

Power Politics: Carbon Energy in Historical Perspective
Clif Stratton, Washington State University

Chronic Disparities: Public Health in Historical Perspective
Sean Wempe, California State University, Bakersfield

Forthcoming

Heavy Traffic: The Global Drug Trade in Historical Perspective
Ken Faunce, Washington State University

Gender Rules: Gender and Empire in Historical Perspective
Karen Phoenix, Washington State University

Ruptured Lives

Refugee Crises in Historical Perspective

Roots of Contemporary Issues

Jesse Spohnholz
Washington State University

New York   Oxford
OXFORD UNIVERSITY PRESS

Oxford University Press is a department of the University of Oxford.
It furthers the University's objective of excellence in research, scholarship,
and education by publishing worldwide. Oxford is a registered trade mark of
Oxford University Press in the UK and certain other countries.

Published in the United States of America by Oxford University Press
198 Madison Avenue, New York, NY 10016, United States of America.

For titles covered by Section 112 of the US Higher Education
Opportunity Act, please visit www.oup.com/us/he for the latest
information about pricing and alternate formats.

Library of Congress Cataloging-in-Publication Data

Names: Spohnholz, Jesse, 1974- author.
Title: Ruptured lives : refugee crises in historical perspective / Jesse
  Spohnholz, Washington State University.
Description: New York : Oxford University Press, 2021. | Series: The roots
  of contemporary issues | Includes bibliographical references and index. |
  Summary: "A higher education history textbook that focuses on refugee
  crises in world history. This is part of the Roots of Contemporary
  Issues series"—Provided by publisher.
Identifiers: LCCN 2020009273 (print) | LCCN 2020009274 (ebook) | ISBN
  9780190696214 (paperback) | ISBN 9780197520598 | ISBN 9780197535332
  (epub) | ISBN 9780190696269
Subjects: LCSH: Refugees—History.
Classification: LCC HV640 .S665 2021 (print) | LCC HV640 (ebook) |
  DDC 362.8709—dc23
LC record available at https://lccn.loc.gov/2020009273
LC ebook record available at https://lccn.loc.gov/2020009274

Printing number: 9 8 7 6 5 4 3 2 1
Printed by LSC Communications, Inc.,
United States of America

CONTENTS

LIST OF MAPS AND FIGURES

Maps

Figures

ABOUT THE AUTHOR

Jesse Spohnholz is Director of the Roots of Contemporary Issues Program and Professor of History at Washington State University. He has researched and published extensively on the experience of refugees, including his prize-winning books, *The Tactics of Toleration: A Refugee Community in the Age of Religious Wars* (2011) and *The Convent of Wesel: The Event That Never Was and the Invention of Tradition* (2017). He teaches courses on world history, European history, historical methods, and the Roots of Contemporary Issues. In addition, he has been recognized with numerous teaching awards, including the William F. Mullen Memorial Teaching Award at Washington State University.

ACKNOWLEDGMENTS

Learning requires unlearning. To write this book, I had to learn and unlearn a lot. I wish to offer my appreciation to a few people who helped me with both. They include colleagues who recommended readings and critiqued drafts, students who exchanged ideas both in and out of the classroom, and friends who served as sounding boards. The original five authors in this book series—Ken Faunce, Karen Phoenix, Clif Stratton, and Sean Wempe—served as a great team in envisioning what the series would look like and helping each other see what any one of us could not see alone. Ken, thanks for your patience and grace. Karen, thanks for taking the initiative. Clif, thanks for having my back. And Sean, thanks for stepping in late and catching up. I also benefited personally and professionally as I wrote this book from the support and collegiality of those faculty most involved with teaching Roots of Contemporary Issues. They include (alphabetically)—besides the above four—Roger Chan, Sung-eun Choi, Kaja Cook, Julian Dodson, Becky Ellis, Philip Guingona, Lawrence Hatter, Michelle Mann, Rob McCoy, Brenna Miller, Sue Peabody, Jennifer Schaefer, Eugene Smelyanksy, Matthew Unangst, Charles Weller, Sarah Walsh, Katy Whalen, Aaron Whelchel, and Ashley Wright. Other colleagues at Washington State University also offered valuable feedback, including Jennifer Binczewski, Steve Fountain, and Steve Kale. I also received useful suggestions, inspiration, and cautions from (again, alphabetically) Ana Barnes, Daniel Fogt, Trevor Getz, Geert Janssen, Carina Johnson, Joshua Johnson, Serena Rex, Nick Terpstra, and Mirjam van Veen, At Oxford University Press, Charles Cavaliere and Katie Tunkavige have provided professional and generous guidance into this new kind of publishing. Thanks also to all the anonymous peer reviewers, who offered invaluable advice. Any remaining errors remain my own. A special thanks too to Sheri Six, for inspiration, guidance, conversation, distraction, perseverance, and so much more.

I owe a particular debt to the 614 students at Washington State University whom I have taught in my the Roots of Contemporary Issues courses so far. I learned—and unlearned—from each of you. I hope I helped you learn and unlearn a little as well. Special thanks go to students in my History 105 classes in the fall of 2016, 2017, and 2018, who were my enthusiastic guinea pigs for the lessons out of which this book emerged.

Connecting Past and Present

Let's begin with events taking place in the last few years. Here's one: in early 2019, Starbucks announced plans to replace plastic straws with recyclable polypropylene lids. "Starbucks is finally drawing a line in the sand and creating a mold for other brands to follow," stated the company's director of packaging. Some supporters see the move as a good example of a market-based solution to environmental damage. Critics warn that it's unlikely that many "green" lids will end up at recycling facilities, since the plan is only slated for stores in two of the seventy-six countries where the company operates, the United States and Canada, which recycle very few polypropylene plastics. Most people agree, though, that plastic pollution has become a problem; worldwide production of plastics in the last few generations has skyrocketed. Many plastics produced today only ever get used for just a few minutes or hours, and then are left for centuries to pollute the earth. Plastics float in enormous masses in our oceans, killing birds, fish, seals, whales, and turtles. They break down into microplastics, making their way into all kinds of organisms. Microplastics found in drinking water are even changing humans' body chemistry. Whose responsibility it is to solve this problem? What solutions are likely to be effective? We will be in a better position to answer those questions if we stop to understand the economic, cultural, political, and social forces that allowed such widespread global plastic pollution to develop in the first place.

Here's another example: On January 28, 2019 the rapper 21 Savage sung a lyric on NBC's *Late Night with Jimmy Fallon* criticizing the US government's policy of separating children from parents who had arrived at the US-Mexico border seeking asylum. A few days later, the US Immigration and Customs Enforcement (ICE) arrested 21 Savage, just a week before the Grammy Awards, for which he had been nominated for his recent collaboration with Post Malone. It turns out the Atlanta-based musician had been brought to the US as a minor by his parents, who failed to renew his visa when it expired. During the Grammys, 21 Savage sat in an ICE detention facility. Supporters of 21 Savage applaud his bringing attention to what they consider an inhumane US immigration policy. Those who disagree with him emphasize the importance of protecting the integrity of national borders and prosecuting violations of American immigration laws. 21 Savage's case became part of a nationwide debate in the US about the arrival of asylum seekers fleeing gang violence in El Salvador, Guatemala, and Honduras, and the US's government's policy of incarcerating children and separating them from their parents. Disagreements on this issue have overlapped with discussions about asylum seekers from the Syrian Civil War as well as about migrants from Latin America who come to the US to work, mostly in the agricultural and service industries, but do not get visas or overstay their visas. But questions about immigration policy and how to response to asylum seekers are by no means limited to the US. In the last couple of years, politicians and ordinary people have been debating similar questions about immigration driven by persecution, poverty, fear of violence, and other hardships in countries such as Lebanon, Turkey, Germany, Britain, India, Bangladesh, Colombia, Brazil, Kenya, and Ethiopia. But too often political dialogue on these issues feels like everyone's goal is to convince others that they are wrong, and treat changing one's mind as a failure rather than as a success. As with the example of plastic, if we work to understand the historical factors that led to these situations, we'll be far better poised to solve problems effectively, instead of contributing to increased polarization.

Here's a third example: a man who murdered over fifty Muslim worshippers in Christchurch, New Zealand in March 2019 was found to have been sharing white nationalist ideas with likeminded people on Facebook and Instagram in the runup to his attack. It turns out that a man who murdered nine African Americans worshipping in a church in Charleston, South Carolina four years earlier had also been using Facebook to exchange hateful and racist ideas with others. Certainly, social media has given people a new platform to spew hate speech, but is there really a relationship between increased racist violence and our new forms of digital communication? After the Christchurch killings, Facebook's executives decided that there was. They announced that the company would remove all white nationalist content from posts on Facebook and its subsidiary, Instagram. Supporters cheered that this massive social media company was taking responsibility to limit hate speech. Critics warned against limiting free speech online. Debate has also centered on whether private companies or governments should be responsible for regulating hate speech and/or protecting free speech. Meanwhile, others worry that extremists are only migrating to new venues, including to the dark web, where they can plot violence free of any oversight. At times one might feel paralyzed by the situation. We want to limit mass violence, but should we accept restrictions on our freedoms to do so? There are other important questions connected to this one. Should anyone be responsible for governing speech on social media? If so, who? And how should do they it? How else could we respond to incidents of mass violence? Often discussions on these topics are guided by people earning ad revenues for every click offering easy-to-understand and/or frantically delivered messages. Fortunately, understanding the longer history of topics like censorship, racism, communication revolutions, and mass violence allows us to take a broader, more mature perspective. Rather than feeling paralyzed, studying the past allows us to make informed decisions about issues and leaves us empowered to help shape the future.

One last example. As the first volumes of this book series entered production in early 2020, a novel coronavirus, which causes the sometimes fatal respiratory illness known as COVID-19, was spreading rapidly throughout the world. First detected in Wuhan, China in late 2019, coronavirus spread to 183 countries and territories in a matter of months. By early April 2020, more than 73,000 people had died, with more than 1.3 million confirmed infections.

In response to this pandemic, national governments have taken uneven measures. South Korea aggressively tested, tracked, and treated in order to slow the spread of the disease. British Prime Minister Boris Johnson faced criticism for his government's more meager response. Johnson delayed the closure of schools, bars, restaurants, museums, and other common gathering spots, even as positive cases in the United Kingdom surpassed 1,300 in mid-March. By early April, Johnson himself landed in intensive care with COVID-19 symptoms.

While we do not yet know the long-term outcomes of the coronavirus pandemic, it has already begun to expose the degree to which the rapid circulation of goods and people throughout the world exposes us all to health threats, even if it does so unevenly. This novel coronavirus has revealed deep global inequities in access to medical care, adequate nutrition, and stable employment that make one more or less likely to contract and survive disease. It has left many societies caught up in a web of just-in-time supply chains woefully underprepared to combat the health threat. The pandemic has exposed the dangers of rapid global travel in spreading disease and highlighted humans' reliance on that same global transportation to share medical supplies and health care personnel. Many advocates of open borders around the world, for example, are supporting border closures to slow the spread of the disease. At least in April 2020, many politicians in the United States seem to be rapidly shifting their positions on policies related to incarceration, debt collection, health care, and guaranteed basic income. The pandemic has also raised important questions about the threats to public health from the intentional and unintentional spread of disinformation. In short order, coronavirus has made us all comprehend just how dependent we are on our fellow humans, for better and for worse. Coronavirus did not create the problems that it has exposed. A purely medical response to the disease will not solve those problems either. But understanding the historical origins of intertwined economic, political, and social developments that shape its spread will put all of us in a better position to address current and future problems rendered acute by disease.

It is the premise of this book series that understanding and addressing the afore-mentioned issues and others facing us today requires understanding their deep and global historical roots. Today's problems are not simply the outcomes of decisions yesterday—they are shaped by years, decades, and centuries of historical developments. A deep historical understanding helps us understand the present-day world in more sophisticated, mature, and reasoned ways. Humans have been interconnected with faraway places for centuries; solving the central problems facing our world means understanding those connections over time.

Too often our popular political dialogue—increasingly driven by social media, partisan politics, and short-term economic interests—ignores or discounts the complex historical dimensions of current issues and thus fails to provide useful contexts for those issues that could help citizens and leaders resolve them. Historians can help their fellow citizens make decisions by explaining the historical developments that created the world we inherited.

Rather than survey all of world history, each book in this series begins in the present with a pressing or seemingly intractable problem facing humanity (i.e., climate change, terrorism, racism, poverty). It then helps us better understand that not only is that problem not intractable but it has historical origins. That is, it has not been a problem since time immemorial, nor is it unique to the present. Rather, problems have historical lives, have undergone changes both subtle and dramatic, and are the outcomes of human decisions and actions. The book in front of you and others in this series will help you: (1) understand the deep historical roots of a pressing and controversial issue facing the world today; (2) understand its global context; (3) interpret evidence to make reasoned, mature conclusions; (4) evaluate the arguments of others surrounding those issues; and (5) identify and utilize research skills to make independent conclusions about contemporary issues of interest to you.

The Case for the Roots of Contemporary Issues

Five central arguments shape this series' scope. First, every book explains why history matters now. Widespread consensus abounds that history helps individuals make reasonable decisions about the present and future. This is why so many governments require that their citizens study history. And yet, in the United States at least, history is pretty consistently among the least popular subjects for high school and college students. Why is this? The answer is probably in part because it is required and because we give so much attention in our society to prioritizing personal and short-term interests, such that studying history seems impractical. Books in this series are explicit about how essential, practical, and empowering studying history is.

Second, all books in the series offer world history, rather than histories of "civilizations" or continents. None of these books, for instance, stops at the history of the "West." There is a good reason for this: the very idea of the "West" only emerged as an effort to imagine a fundamental civilizational distinctiveness that has never existed. The "West" developed in response to interactions between people in Europe and North America with peoples around the world. The "West" offered a politically motivated myth of a linear inheritance from Greece and Rome to modern Europe, and from modern Europe to the United States. But many facts had to be omitted (intentionally or unintentionally) to sustain that argument.

The idea of the "West" had its core in some kind of definition of Europe, and tacked on the majority-white populations in settler colonies in North America, Australia, and elsewhere. That is, the definition of the "West" is rooted in ideas about race and in global racism, which were not just products of internal developments (i.e., developments taking place exclusively within Europe and the United States), but also of the centuries-long interactions of people around the globe, including systems of colonialism and slavery. In short, these volumes recognize that humans have interacted across large spaces for centuries, and that many of the geographical terms that we use to understand the world—the West, Middle East, the Far East, Europe, America, Africa—only came to exist as products of those interactions.

Third, while all volumes in the series offer world histories, they are also different from most world histories in that they focus on the history of a specific issue. In our view, a central challenge facing a lot of world history is the magnitude of coverage required by adopting a global scope. Some solve this problem by dividing up the world into continents. That approach can be effective, but suffers from the same challenge as books that adopt civilizational paradigms like "the West." Others attempt to solve the problem by adopting global narratives that replace older civilizational ones. Global approaches can help us see patterns previously overlooked, but risk erasing the complexity of human experiences and decisions in order to tell universalizing stories that can make the outcomes look inevitable. They often do not capture the extent to which even major outcomes—political revolutions, technological changes, economic transformations—are the products of decisions made by ordinary people. Neither can they capture the logical counterpoint: that those people could have made other decisions, and that ordinary people actually do transform the world every day.

The fourth argument that shapes the scope of this series relates to the interconnection between premodern and modern history. What does "modern" signify in the first place? Most understandings of the past rely on this concept, but its meaning is notoriously hard to pin down. One easy way to think about the options is to look at how historians have divided up history into premodern and modern eras in textbooks and classes.

One common dividing point is 1500. The argument here is that a set of shifts between roughly 1450 and 1550 fundamentally transformed the world so that the periods before and after this period can be understood as distinct from one another. These include global explorations, the information revolution associated with the invention of the printing press, a set of military campaigns that established the boundaries of lands ruled by Muslim and Christian princes, and the spread of Renaissance capitalism.

Another common dividing point between the modern and premodern is 1800. Critical here are the development of industrial production and transportation, democratic forms of governance, waves of anticolonial revolutions in the Americas, novel forms of Western imperialism that came to dominate much of Africa and Asia, the intensification of scientific understandings of the world, and the spread of new secular ideologies, like nationalism. There are other dividing points that historians have used to separate history, but these two are the most common.

Regardless of which breaking point you find most convincing, there are at least two problems with this way of dividing histories along "modern" and "premodern" lines. First, these divisions are usually Eurocentric in orientation. They presuppose that "modernity" was invented in Europe, and then exported elsewhere. As a result, peoples whose histories are divided up differently or that are less marked by European norms wrongly appear "backward." The second problem with these divisions is that they are less capable of identifying continuities across these divides.

We are not arguing that distinguishing between "modern" and "premodern" is always problematic. Rather, we see advantages to framing histories *across* these divides. Histories that only cover the modern period sometimes simplify the premodern world or treat people who lived long ago as irrelevant, often missing important early legacies. Meanwhile, histories that only cover premodern periods often suffer because their relevance for understanding the present is hard to see. They sometimes ask questions of interest to only professional historians with specialized knowledge. This series seeks to correct for each of these problems by looking for premodern inheritances in the modern world.

The final argument that shapes the series is that we have a stronger understanding of developments when we study the interrelationships between large structures of power, processes of change, and individual responses to both. The books work to help you understand how history has unfolded by examining the past from these three interactive perspectives. The first is structural: how political, economic, social, and, cultural power functioned at specific times and places. The second explains what forces have led to transformations from one condition to another. The third looks at how individuals have responded to both structures and changes, including how they resisted structures of power in ways that promoted change.

Historians distinguish between structure, change, and agency. Leaving out agency can make structures and changes look inevitable. Leaving out change flattens out the world, as if it were always the same (hint: always be skeptical of a sentence that begins with: "Throughout history"!). Leaving out structures celebrates human choices and autonomy, but naively ignores how broader contexts limit or shape our options. Understanding how structure, change, and agency interact allows us to create a more realistic picture of how the world works.

Doing History

When we talk to authors about writing these books, we urge that they do not need to provide all the answers to the issues that they write about, but should instead provide readers with the skills to find answers for themselves. That is, using the goals just described, this series is meant to help you think more critically about the relationship between the past and the present by developing discrete but mutually reinforcing research and analytical skills.

First, the volumes in this series will help you learn how to ask critical historical questions about contemporary issues—questions that do not beg simplistic answers but instead probe more deeply into the past, bridge seemingly disconnected geographies, and recognize the variety of human experiences. Second, you will learn how to assess, integrate, and compare the arguments of scholars who study both historical and contemporary issues. Historians do not always agree about cause and effect, the relative importance of certain contributing factors over others, or even how best to interpret a single document. This series will help you understand the importance of these debates and to find your own voice within them.

Third, you will learn how to identify, evaluate, interpret, and organize varieties of primary sources—evidence that comes from the periods you are studying—related to specific historical processes. Primary sources are the raw evidence contained in the historical record, produced at the time of an event or process either by a person or group of people directly involved or by a first-hand observer. Primary sources nearly always require historians to analyze and present their larger significance. As such, you will learn how to develop appropriate historical contexts within which to situate primary sources.

While we listed these three sets of skills in order, in fact you might begin with any one of them. For example, you may already have a historical question in mind after reading several recent news articles about a contemporary problem.

That question would allow you to begin searching for appropriate debates about the historical origins of that problem or to seek out primary sources for analysis. Conversely, you might begin searching for primary sources on a topic of interest to you and then use those primary sources to frame your question. Likewise, you may start with an understanding of two opposing viewpoints about the historical origins of the problem and then conduct your own investigation into the evidence to determine which viewpoint ultimately holds up.

But only after you have developed each of these skills will you be in a position to practice a fourth critical skill: producing analytical arguments backed by historical evidence and situated within appropriate scholarly debates and historical contexts. Posing such arguments will allow you to make reasoned, mature conclusions about how history helps us all address societal problems with that same reason and maturity. We have asked authors to model and at times talk through these skills as they pertain to the issue they have contributed to the series.

Series Organization

Each volume in this series falls under one of five primary themes in history. None attempt to offer a comprehensive treatment of all facets of a theme but instead will expose you to more specific and focused histories and questions clearly relevant to understanding the past's impact on the present.

The first theme—Humans and the Environment—investigates how we have interacted with the natural world over time. It considers how the environment shapes human life, but also how humans have impacted the environment by examining economic, social, cultural, and political developments. The second theme, Globalization, allows us to put our relationship to the natural world into a greater sense of motion. It explores the transformations that have occurred as human relationships have developed across vast distances over centuries. The third theme, the Roots of Inequality, explores the great disparities (the "haves" and "have-nots") of the world around us, along lines of race, gender, class, or other differences. This approach allows us to ask questions about the origins of inequality, and how the inequalities in the world today relate to earlier eras, including the past five hundred years of globalization.

Diverse Ways of Thinking, the fourth theme, helps us understand the past's diverse peoples on their own terms and to get a sense of how they understood one another and the world around them. It addresses the historical nature of ideologies and worldviews that people have developed to conceptualize the differences and inequalities addressed in the inequality theme. The fifth theme, the Roots of Contemporary Conflicts, explores the historical roots of conflicts rooted in diverse worldviews, environmental change, inequalities, and global interactions over time. Its goal is to illuminate the global and local factors that help explain specific conflicts. It often integrates elements of the previous four themes within a set of case studies rooted in the past but also helps explain the dramatic changes we experience and/or witness in the present.

Our thematic organization is meant to provide coherence and structure to a series intended to keep up with global developments in the present as historians work to provide essential contexts for making sense of those developments. Every subject facing the world today—from responding to COVID-19 to debates about the death penalty, from transgender rights to coal production, and from the Boko Haram rebellion in Nigeria to micro-aggressions in Massachusetts—can be better understood by considering the topic in the context of world history.

History is not a path toward easy solutions: we cannot simply copy the recommendations of Mohandas Gandhi, Sojourner Truth, Karl Marx, Ibn Rushd, or anyone else for that matter, to solve problems today. To do so would be foolhardy. But we can better understand the complex nature of the problems we face so that the solutions we develop are mature, responsible, thoughtful, and informed. In the following book, we have asked one historian with specialized knowledge and training in this approach to guide you through this process for one specific urgent issue facing the world.

—Jesse Spohnholz and Clif Stratton

ROOTS OF CONTEMPORARY ISSUES

RUPTURED LIVES

INTRODUCTION

When I started writing this book, in 2016, people around the world were debating how to respond to the Syrian refugee crisis. At the time, Europeans, Americans, Australians, and others in the Western world were deliberating whether to welcome asylum seekers fleeing war-torn Syria. At the height of these discussions, considerable misinformation circulated among politicians, on social media, around family dinner tables, and among friends. Sometimes Westerners cast blame on just a few individuals, simplifying a complex history into a tale of villains and martyrs. Meanwhile, most Syrian refugees were not fleeing to the West. Eighty to ninety percent of these waves of more than six million refugees escaped to neighboring states like Turkey, Lebanon, Jordan, and Iraq. Today, this humanitarian crisis in the Middle East remains among the gravest in the world, and is transforming politics in the region.

Since then, other refugee crises around the world have commanded attention as well.[1] In 2019, the United Nations reported that over 700,000 Rohingya refugees fleeing ethnic violence in Myanmar were living in refugee camps in neighboring Bangladesh and elsewhere. The ongoing conflicts in the Democratic Republic of the Congo have led over 800,000 people to flee. As I write these words, the refugee crisis commanding the most attention in the United States involves people fleeing war, gangs, and poverty in Guatemala, El Salvador, and Honduras. In all, there are over twenty-five million refugees around the world today. By the time that you read this book, refugee flows may have intensified or transformed, but it's unlikely that you've seen their disappearance.

Much of the world's politics today revolves around questions about refugees and other migrating peoples, including debating the scope and limits of humanitarianism, the relevance of national borders in a globalized world, racist rhetoric

---

1. See United Nations High Commissioner for Refugees, provided at https://www.unhcr.org/en-us/.

and policies, global economic inequalities, and worldwide environmental disasters. There are no easy answers to these questions, though the decisions that all of us make about them will have tremendous consequences for individuals and for the planet. It is the premise of this book that studying the history of refugee crises can help us make those decisions more responsibly.

The goal of this book is not to explain every refugee crisis that has ever existed. Neither is it to overwhelm you with the hardships of the oppressed, with a goal of motivating you to take a particular action that I recommend. I don't have the answers for what to do, I am sad to say. But I can offer useful perspectives by looking at the past. Thus, my goal is to provide an intellectual framework for understanding how to think about the conflicts that produce refugees and the effects that refugee crises have on individuals and societies. This book is centrally about *conflicts* that have produced migrations of people fleeing dangers or persecution. It is not centrally about all migrations, all forced migrations, or even all refugee movements. There are no climate refugees in this book, for instance, though it seems likely that we'll see more of them as the twenty-first century sputters on.[2] Instead, this book is about specific kinds of dramatic refugee migrations that emerged out of debates about what kind of people deserve to live in what areas of our planet.

Refugees and Crises

In order to explain what I mean, let me define my terms. I take a "refugee" to be a person who flees one's place (or places) of residence out of fear of ongoing or anticipated hardships that pose a serious threat to life, safety, or means of supporting oneself or one's family. I modeled my definition in part on that provided by the United Nations, which states that a refugee is any person who

> owing to well-founded fear of being persecuted for reasons of race, religion, nationality, membership of a particular social group or political opinion, is outside the country of his nationality and is unable or, owing to such fear, is unwilling to avail himself of the protection of that country; or who, not having a nationality and being outside the country of his former habitual residence as a result of such events, is unable or, owing to such fear, is unwilling to return to it.[3]

---

2. Interested in learning more? One useful start is Harald Welzer, *Climate Wars: What People Will Be Killed For in the 21st Century* (Malden, MA: Polity Press, 2012).

3. This language comes from the 1951 Convention and Protocol Relating to the Status of Refugees, as amended in 1967, https://www.unhcr.org/en-my/4ae57b489.pdf.

My definition follows the spirit of the United Nations', but is less precise.[4] Detailed definitions can prove helpful for answering questions about human rights. However, they can also obscure complex historical realities that I seek to understand. My definition, for instance, does not define what types of fears define the legitimacy of one's refugee status. Of course, I only have that freedom because I'm not responsible for the urgent task of distributing aid or making judgments of international law. But that separation also allows me to explain historical events more completely, including appreciating the multiple, overlapping reasons that people have fled.

Consider the distinction between refugees and economic migrants. The United Nations' definition excludes economic reasons for claiming refugee status. Some Western politicians today use this distinction between economic migrants and those they describe as legitimate asylum seekers in order to limit the number of migrants admitted to their country. But when studying the history of refugees, this distinction sometimes confuses more than it clarifies. First, people sometimes fled for more than one reason. Refugees may have fled out of fear of being persecuted, but their inability to earn a living because of war and violence surely also played a factor as well. Trying to get into an individual's decision-making process—which reason was the "real" reason a person left—can be a fruitless exercise. In research for an earlier book, I also discovered refugees who overemphasized economic reasons for their migration to avoid getting a reputation as extremists as well as those who exaggerated the religious persecution they faced in order to elicit sympathy.[5] But these were rhetorical strategies used in times of hardship, not windows into their decision-making process. In many cases, we simply have no evidence either way for specific individuals. While some policymakers and politicians today seek to delegitimize a refugee's status as an asylum seeker by pointing to economic advantages for migration, this book does not pretend there are clear lines to be drawn. At the same time, the book limits itself to refugees, according to my definition. It does not explore the more general phenomenon of economic migration (documented or undocumented) from poorer to wealthier regions of the world, which deserves its own treatment.

At times in this book, I find it helpful to distinguish between "exiles" and "refugees." Exiles are people who have been explicitly banned from a territory, while refugee is a more general term for any person who has fled out of fear of danger. From the perspective of both their home and host territories, the distinction might be important in determining property rights or asylum status. But

---

4. I also avoid gender-specific language, though this is a matter of changing writing conventions in the past seventy years, rather than a substantive disagreement about who counts as a refugee.

5. Jesse Spohnholz, *The Tactics of Toleration: A Refugee Community in the Age of Religious Wars* (Newark: University of Delaware Press, 2011).

here again we need to exercise both caution and flexibility. It can sometimes be hard for a historian to tell the difference in practice. One group of people might have been explicitly exiled, but others who were not exiled may have fled with them out of reasonable fear for their own safety. Exiles and other refugees often lived together, intermarried, and built social relationships. In other cases, the legal status of a refugee was unclear or unknown at the time, or was known then but cannot be determined today. Thus, while this book distinguishes between exiles and refugees in cases where it proves helpful, it recognizes that making rigid distinctions sometimes obscures the lived realities of refugees.

I should also explain what I mean by using the term "crisis." Today, supporters of more restrictive policies toward immigration often use the term to exaggerate the risk that asylum seekers pose to them or their culture. Often when they use this rhetoric, they employ racist tropes that suggest that migrants who look or think differently than themselves somehow pose fundamental threats to their well-being. From the standpoint of a historian, this perspective is problematic because it imagines cultures and societies as disconnected from one another and unchanging over time. Historians understand that cultural changes and the movement of peoples have been taking place since the start of human history. Thus, I don't use the term "crisis" in this way. Instead, by refugee crises, I mean mass migrations that are abrupt and large enough that they reveal compelling insights about home communities, migrants, and hosts. That is, I use the term "crisis" to describe a historical phenomenon, not to comment on the outcomes of those events. As we'll see, the outcomes of refugee crises could be extremely diverse. My aim has been to look for patterns that explain the various causes and outcomes for refugee crises.

Big Ideas and Ruptured Lives

In order to understand the causes and effects of refugee crises in world history, this book uses the concepts of "big ideas" and "ruptured lives." By *big ideas* I refer to the development and spread of assumptions that underpin people's worldviews so strongly that they come to believe that they are fundamental to the world order, even though they are actually products of historical developments. Each chapter includes a reflection on a big idea in history. One of the most important kinds of big ideas relates to what scholars call metageography. What does that mean? Metageography refers to a set of conscious or unconscious ideas that people have about the relationships between geographical spaces and the humans inhabiting those spaces. There are two forms of metageography that I use to organize this book. The first is the "myth of continents."[6] The idea is simple: most of us learn from

6. Kären Wigen and Martin W. Lewis, *The Myth of Continents: A Critique of Metageography* (Berkeley: University of California Press, 1997).

a young age that there are seven continents, though how we divide up the spaces of the earth is as much about historical developments as it is about geology. Europe, the Americas, Asia, and Africa are not just self-evident geological features. They are ideas that carry assumptions about what kinds of people live (or should live) in those geographical spaces and what kinds of people do not (or should not). The second metageography guiding this book is the "invention of traditions" required for the emergence of nation-states.[7] As we will learn, nation-states are not the expression of some timeless soul of a preexisting ancient people, but the products of historical developments that led some people to imagine themselves as bound to one another. In cases when their borders stabilized, they also came to be places in which individuals and groups imagined what kinds of people should (or could) live within those borders, and what kinds of people should (or could) not. This book argues that metageographies of continents and invented national traditions are helpful to understand some of the most impactful refugee crises in world history.

Central to this book's premise about big ideas is that to make sense of the conflicts that create refugee crises, we need to examine the worldviews of the people who have committed coercion and violence from a sympathetic perspective. The point is not to condone or excuse persecution. Rather, it is to understand how it is that real human beings—people with families and loved ones, cherished values, insecurities about their appearance, and other human characteristics that you and I share—can decide that their best course of action is to perpetrate violence. The committers of violence in the histories told in this book were not psychotics or sociopaths. Their violence followed a certain logic, though one that probably rested on different assumptions than your own. But because they imagined their worldviews as perfectly rational, perpetrators could commit violence relatively guilt free. In order to comprehend their actions, we need to study the historical context in which those people lived, and try to understand their worldviews from their perspectives, even if we find it repulsive or alien. We also need to approach the refugees sympathetically, without succumbing to the lure of treating them all as helpless victims or heroic martyrs. Our goal, that is, must be to appreciate the complex humanity of persecutors, refugees, and hosts alike.

If every chapter introduces a big idea, each one also looks at conflicts that emerged out of disputes over those big ideas, and the refugee crises that resulted. For each, I looked for "push factors" (those causing people to flee) and "pull factors" (those drawing people to certain locations). I also avoided the assumption that all refugees in a particular crisis experienced ruptures in the same way. As such, I looked for evidence for how different kinds of people (of different religions, ethnicities, ages, and genders) experienced refugee crises. I also tried to distinguish between the short- and long-term consequences of refugee crises.

---

7. Eric Hobsbawm and Terence Ranger, eds., *The Invention of Tradition* (Cambridge: Cambridge University Press, 1983).

I didn't assume that refugees are always innocent victims. Or that experiencing persecution necessarily promoted radicalization. Or that the cultures that existed before their migrations were pristine and idyllic. Or that losing one's home inherently meant traumatic loss. Or that cultural change is fundamentally bad. One of my goals in writing this book has been to challenge these clichés. In examining these "ruptured lives," I aim to tell the history of these refugee crises without trivializing or characterizing them using simplistic soundbites of good and evil.

Chapter Summary

Commenters on refugee crises often only take a short-term view of the conflicts that produced them. This book is organized around "big ideas" and "ruptured lives" as a corrective. It explains how developments going back centuries produced metageographies that also help us better understand some of the most dramatic refugee crises in world history. The book begins its first chapter by exploring the history of the myth of continents for the kinds of people who were most responsible for inventing the metageographies that we find through the rest of the book: Europeans. The point is not to replicate the very Eurocentrism that Clif Stratton and I critiqued in the introduction to this book series. Rather, it is to highlight the distinction between the complex lived realities of human beings and the fictional, universalist myth that Western norms define modernity. Thus, this book highlights the constructed nature of Europe, recognizes the powerful influence of Western colonialism on world history, and moves us beyond Eurocentric metageographies that mistakenly shape the assumptions of many people all over the world, even today.[8]

Chapter 1 argues that the rupture of an earlier idea—the idea of Christendom—underpinned a set of refugee crises on the large peninsula that today we call Europe during the early modern era (c. 1450–c. 1750). It follows Protestants, Catholics, Jews, and Muslims who escaped persecution and wars and describes two locations—the Ottoman Empire and the Dutch Republic— that became especially receptive to integrating refugees. It ends by explaining how these developments led to the creation of a new idea of Europe by the mid-eighteenth century. Though Europeans have not been responsible for all metageographies in world history by any means, the processes that related to the invention of Europe—especially colonialism and nation building—proved central to other metageographies covered in this book.

---

8. Two books that influenced my thinking are Dipesh Chakrabarty, *Provincializing Europe: Postcolonial Thought and Historical Differences*, 2nd ed. (Princeton, NJ: Princeton University Press, 2008); Prasenjit Duara, *Rescuing History from the Nation: Questioning Narratives of Modern China* (Chicago: University of Chicago Press, 1999).

Chapter 2 explores refugee crises that resulted from European colonization of the Americas during the same time period. It begins by describing the invention of the idea of America as embedded in assumptions about the legitimacy of European cultural superiority and political domination. The chapter identifies refugees who fled from Europe to the Americas, including English Puritans, French Huguenots, Jews, and Muslims. However, it argues that we find far more significant refugee crises among people in the African diaspora escaping slavery and displaced indigenous Americans fleeing war, enslavement, and dislocations as a result of European colonialism. Native American and African refugees built new hybrid societies across the Americas, some of which challenged European domination while others only strengthened colonialism.

Chapter 3 focuses on the creation of nation-states in the nineteenth century and the refugee crises that emerged as a result during and immediately after World War I (1914–1923). It explains the invention of nation-states, another "big idea" that played a critical role in sparking the most devastating war yet in world history. The conflict itself sparked massive refugee crises in Europe and western Asia, which in some cases dramatically intensified ethnic nationalism. After the war, the victors chopped up formerly multiethnic empires into ethnically defined nation-states, which sparked a further round of refugee crises. The chapter concludes by briefly comparing the refugee crises of World War I to those of World War II.

Chapter 4 examines how the introduction of nations-states in "Asia"— another big idea—combined to create refugee crises in former European colonies after World War II (1945–1950). I focus on two case studies: Israel/Palestine and India/Pakistan. The case of Israel/Palestine involves the creation of a Western-style nation-state in the lands of the former Ottoman Empire. A critical feature of the crises there was that the Jewish refugees moving to Israel and Palestinian refugees fleeing from it both saw themselves as victimized martyrs. The case of India/Pakistan involves another sudden creation of nation-states that saw violence as a result of resentments that had built up during the colonial era. Muslim refugees fled to Pakistan while Hindu and Sikh refugees fled to India, in what was perhaps the largest population transfer in world history. The chapter ends with a brief discussion of the refugee crisis in the Korean peninsula in order to highlight the late 1940s as a particularly unstable time in this region.

The final chapter focuses on the relationship between diverse ideas about "Africa"—our last big idea—and three refugee crises in Algeria, Uganda, and Africa's Great Lakes Region during the second half of the twentieth century (1950s–1990s). In Algeria, anticolonial activists called for Africans to unite against colonial rule during the brutal Algerian War, which saw refugee crises during and after the fighting. In Uganda, in the name of returning Africa to Africans, antagonisms toward residents who were part of the Indian diaspora led to the mass expulsion of the so-called Asian population. And in Africa's Great Lakes Region, colonialism entrenched a racialized distinction between supposedly indigenous African Hutus and supposedly foreign Tutsis that erupted into cycles of conflict and refugee crises that spanned the countries of Rwanda, Burundi, Uganda, the Democratic Republic of the Congo, and Tanzania. The legacies of all the refugee crises covered in this book continue to have resonances today.

Sources and Methods

How did I go about writing this book? For many people, such a project might seem intimidating. At first, it was for me too. If you are reading this book as part of an introductory history course that has a research component, then perhaps you'll understand the feeling. Having a plan helped. My first step was basic: I searched in my university library's database for recently written books that covered the history of refugees and migrations from a broad geographical and chronological perspective.[9] I read those (and took careful notes), and then mined their footnotes and bibliographies for more suggestions for my reading list. Then I searched my library for general histories of the regions I was studying. These books were not about refugees themselves, but scholarly overviews that provided an introduction to nonspecialists of the history of a continent, country, or time period.[10] As I read, I learned some of the terminology and names that would be necessary to read scholarly articles, other specialized publications, and primary sources that I read later. I also asked history professors for help. That proved extremely practical because I could explain my interests to a human being, which proved more efficient (and enjoyable) than trying to explain them to a library search engine! Those experts corrected my misunderstandings, but also offered me suggestions for readings that I would never have found otherwise. In time, I collected enough notes on the topics that I started to see patterns in the evidence. After many more conversations with students and colleagues, I finally felt I could build an argument from evidence. The result is the book you are now reading. It includes some troubling stories, to be sure, but ones that help us better understand the world we have inherited.

---

9. Two proved particularly helpful, Peter Gatrell, *The Making of the Modern Refugee* (Oxford: Oxford University Press, 2013); Dirk Hoerder, *Cultures in Contact: World Migrations in the Second Millenium* (Durham, NC: Duke University Press, 2002).

10. Here's one example of what I mean for each chapter. Mark Greengrass, *Christendom Destroyed: Europe, 1517–1648* (New York: Penguin, 2014); Alan Taylor, *American Colonies: The Settling of North America* (New York: Penguin, 2001); E. J. Hobsbawm, *The Age of Revolution, 1789–1848*, 1st Vintage Books ed. (New York: Vintage Books, 1996); Barbara Metcalf and Thomas Metcalf, *A Concise History of Modern India*, 2nd ed. (Cambridge: Cambridge University Press, 2006); Guy Arnold, *Africa: A Modern History, 1945–2015* (London: Atlantic Books, 2005).

1

REFORMATION, REFUGEES, AND THE CREATION OF EUROPE

In 1756 the French philosopher Jean-Jacques Rousseau wrote these intriguing words:

> It cannot be denied that Europe, even now, is indebted more to Christianity than to any other influence . . . So true is this that the one nation which has refused to accept Christianity has always remained an alien among the rest. Christianity, so despised in its infancy, ended by serving as a sanctuary to its slanderers. And the Roman Empire, which had persecuted it for centuries with fruitless cruelty, drew from it a power which she could no longer find in her own strength. The missionaries did more for her than any [military] victory.[1]

I want to begin this chapter by reflecting on Rousseau's words. Writing during the era of Enlightenment, Rousseau promoted a secular philosophy of government and civil society that many have credited with shaping European politics up until today. Why was it that he

---

1. Jean-Jacques Rousseau, *A Lasting Peace through the Federation of Europe and The State of War*, trans. Charles Edwyn Vaughan (London: Constable and Co., 1917), 42–43.

suggested that the history of Christianity was so critical to the very existence of Europe? To answer this question, let's consider a fact that may contradict what you learned in grade school: Europe is not a continent. Take a look at it on a map (Map 1.1). Geographically speaking, it is only a large peninsula of the earth's

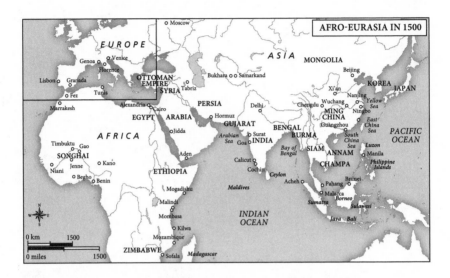

MAP 1.1 Afro-Eurasia in 1500

largest landmass (that is, Asia). No good argument based on geography alone can reasonably be made that Europe is a distinct continent. If Europe doesn't exist geologically, what is it? The answer is that Europe is *an* idea that emerged as the product of historical events. This is our first lesson in metageography, our first "big idea."

The history of the idea of Europe is critical to understanding much of the world today, because so many of the metageographies in world history bear some relationship to the idea of Europe, an idea so deeply mythologized that some people seem incapable of thinking outside of European norms. This chapter thus begins our venture into metageographies in world history by offering two related arguments. The first is that a set of historical events and decisions gradually over centuries—quite unintentionally—had the result of creating the idea of Europe. By the time that Rousseau was writing, Europe had developed its present-day meaning: a collection of states situated in a distinct geographical region with shared characteristics and relationships that their inhabitants believed (sometimes falsely) distinguished them from other regions of the world. Creating this new idea of Europe, however, required dismantling another big idea that had long been dominant in the same region—the idea of Christendom. The second argument of this chapter is that the transformation from one metageography (Christendom) to another (Europe) resulted in profound political instabilities and social fissures that ignited refugee crises that were the result of an impossible dream of achieving religious purity during an age of intense religious difference.

The Creation of Christendom

In the ancient world, the geographical feature that gave rise to a shared culture in this region was not made of land but water: by the first century CE the Roman Empire effectively encircled the Mediterranean Sea. Residents of the city of Rome saw themselves closely bound to people living in modern-day Libya and Lebanon, and not to Celts or Danes to their north. The word Europe, I should note, *was* an ancient one. It comes from *Europa*, a mythical Phoenician princess who supposedly became queen of Crete. Ancient Greeks used the term geographically. The philosopher Aristotle (384–322 BCE) distinguished between peoples living to his north and west in "Europe" and peoples living to his east in "Asia."[2] But no one referred to themselves as Europeans and no people imagined that they lived in a place called Europe.

A critical precondition for the creation of Christendom was the Roman Empire's adoption of Christianity as its official religion. The Emperor Constantine's legalization of Christianity in 313 CE marks a convenient turning

---

2. Aristotle, *The Politics*, trans. Carnes Lord (Chicago: University of Chicago Press, 1984), 208.

point, but more important yet were the policies of Emperor Theodosius I in the 380s and 390s, which made Christianity the only legal religion in the empire. In the years that followed, Christianity spread rapidly. This is what Rousseau meant when he suggested that the Roman Empire had drawn from Christianity, "a power which she could no longer find in her own strength." While Rousseau assumed that Christianity spread primarily through missionary activity, scholars now understand that political and economic factors played a critical role in spreading the religion too.[3] By the 400s and 500s, Christianity was turning from a minority religion that faced persecution into a majority religion that was intolerant of people of other faiths. Roman theologians like Augustine of Hippo found justification for intolerance in scriptural passages like the parable of the banquet in the Gospel of Luke (chapter 14: 21–23), in which Jesus describes a master instructing his servant to compel others to join. In a letter he wrote in 408 CE to Vincent, a pacifist bishop from the North African city of Cartennae (in present-day Algeria), Augustine wrote:

> Do you think no one should be forced to do right, when you read that the master of the house said to his servants: "Whomever you find, compel them to come in"; when you read also that Saul himself, afterward Paul, was forced by the great violence of Christ's compulsion to acknowledge and hold the truth . . . Or do you think that no force should be used to free a man from destructive error, when you see, by the most convincing examples, that God Himself does this—and no one loves us more advantageously than He does.[4]

In cases when it served God's truth, Augustine concluded, persecution is the right answer. While Augustine defended the use of coercion to spread his faith, he also denied that Christianity had any claim to a specific territory. Instead, he distinguished between the so-called City of Man, which might have earthly territory, and the City of God, which was only eternal and heavenly.

Though Augustine never intended it, a process that we might call the territorialization of Christianity turned out to be a consequence of the tight link that emerged between political authority and religious membership in the late Roman Empire. Christians started mapping their sacred geography onto biblical stories. A common way that they did this was by borrowing a distinction made by the first-century Jewish scholar Flavius Josephus in describing the peopling of the

3. See W. V. Harris, ed. *The Spread of Christianity in the First Four Centuries: Essays in Explanation* (Leiden: Brill, 2005).

4. Saint Augustine, *Letters*, vol. 2, translated by Winfried Parsons (Washington, DC: The Catholic University of America Press), 60–61.

earth after Yahweh flooded the earth, a story told in the Hebrew Bible. According to Josephus, Noah's three sons spread in different directions: from Noah's landing site—which he believed was in present-day Armenia—Japheth headed west (as far as present-day Spain), Shem went east (toward present-day Iran and India), and Ham traveled south (toward present-day Egypt and beyond). By the 600s, many Christian thinkers associated the lands of Japheth with Christendom, Shem with Asia and Judaism, and Ham with Africa.[5]

Meanwhile, the Roman Empire was slowly collapsing. In the eastern Mediterranean the empire became so diminished that historians usually distinguish it by calling it the Byzantine Empire. In the 600s and 700s, large swaths of land in the eastern Mediterranean, North Africa, and Iberia were captured by Arabic-speaking Muslims, who usually granted non-Muslims religious freedoms if they paid taxes and otherwise obeyed the law. Across much of the Roman Empire's former northern and western territories, a series of Germanic kingdoms emerged, in which rulers maintained the empire's intolerant logic. Germanic kings also spread Christianity to lands as far away as Scandinavia and Russia that had never fallen under Roman rule, in part because missionaries were willing to integrate non-Christian beliefs and practices, including ideas about magic and astrology.[6] While politically the lands remained decentralized, religiously they developed a coherence in their residents' widespread allegiance to Christianity. Many Christians developed a belief—one quite alien to Augustine—that Christianity had a specific earthly territory—an idea conveyed by the word *Christendom*. When people first began to use the word "Europe" to describe the place where they lived, they treated it as a synonym for "Christendom," as when the Irish monk Columba called the Roman pope the "most fair Head of all the Churches in the whole of Europe."[7] That is, after the fall of the Roman Empire, many Christians territorialized their faith. Yet they did not imagine their religion's geographic space as fixed. After all, their goal was to expand Christendom—and with it the salvation of souls—over the whole world.

One historian, R. I. Moore, has argued that starting about the 1200s, this version of Christendom constituted a "persecuting society."[8] The phrase is useful,

---

5. Denys Hay, *Europe: The Emergence of an Idea* (Edinburgh: Edinburgh University Press, 1957), 1–15.

6. Valerie I. J. Flint, *The Rise of Magic in Early Medieval Europe* (Prineton, NJ: Princeton University Press, 1991).

7. "*Pulcherrimo omnium totius Europae Ecclesiarum Capiti.*" *Santi Columbani Opera*, edited by G. S. M. Walker (Dublin: The Dublin Institute for Advanced Studies, 1970), 36–37. Cited in Karl Leyser, "Concepts of Europe in the Early and High Middle Ages," in *Communications and Power in Medieval Europe*, ed. Timothy Reuter (London: Hambledon Press, 1994), 5.

8. R. I. Moore, *The Formation of a Persecuting Society: Authority and Deviance in Western Europe, 950–1250* (Malden, MA: Blackwell, 2007).

but needs to be treated with care. Another historian, Cary Nederman, has pointed out that literate elites were not unanimous in their intolerance.[9] Also, persecution did not necessarily aim to eradicate difference. Consider the example of annual attacks on Jews in medieval Iberia during Holy Week, studied by David Nirenberg.[10] One week a year, ritualized attacks on Jews reminded them of their subordinate place. The violence did not aim to eliminate religious minorities, but to reinforce hierarchies of power. The situation was intolerant, for sure, though the example reminds us that there are different magnitudes and forms of intolerance. Still, Moore's idea of a "persecuting society" is valuable in that it shows that governments adopted an intolerant version of Christianity not as a result of the intrinsic backwardness of the Middle Ages but as the result of historical processes, including the emergence of kingdoms that borrowed forms of law, culture, and religion from Christian Rome.

It took a millennium before the boundaries of Christendom approximately matched the lands that today we call Europe. There was nothing inevitable about the outcome. Europe was not a preexisting form waiting to be "discovered." Rather, thousands of decisions made by all sorts of people compounded over centuries, such that the lands that today we associate with Europe were approximately set by 1500. Historians will never know every decision that was part of this process, but here we can touch on a few of the most important.

One key development was the division of the Church of Rome from the Eastern Orthodox Church. The origins of this schism can be found in 300 CE, when Emperor Constantine moved the empire's capital to a Greek-speaking city (now renamed Constantinople in his honor). Constantine's decision promoted a cultural gap between the poorer and less stable Latin-speaking western empire and the wealthier and more powerful Greek-speaking east. That gap widened in the early 700s, when Emperor Leo III (r. 717–741) came to believe that the Christian Church was going astray in its extensive use of images, which he felt betrayed the First Commandment. In 726 he banned images from the empire's churches. The strongest opposition to this move came from the pope in Rome, Gregory II (r. 715–731), who warned that defenders of images would turn to Germanic kingdoms for support unless Leo revoked his decree. That's exactly what happened. His successor Gregory III (r. 731–741) allied with Germanic Lombards and Franks against the Byzantines. These alliances helped Germanic kings consolidate power, but also loosened the ties between Rome and Constantinople. A century later, the Eastern Church reversed its position on religious imagery,

9. Cary J. Nederman, *Worlds of Difference: European Discourses of Toleration, c. 1100–c. 1550* (University Park: The Pennsylvania State University Press, 2000).

10. David Nirenberg, *Communities of Violence: Persecution of Minorities in the Middle Ages* (Princeton, NJ: Princeton University Press, 1995), 200–30.

but the gulf remained. In the east, the church developed strong ties to Greek culture and an alliance with the emperor in Constantinople. In the west, an array of Germanic rulers allied with the pope of the Latin-speaking church in Rome. By 1054 the Patriarch Michael I Cerularius and Pope Leo IX excommunicated one another. If the lands that today we call Europe include all the areas where Christianity was dominant by the mid- to late-fifteenth century, the boundary of the 1054 schism roughly matches the line that mapmakers make between Eastern and Western Europe.

The Christian crusades of the late eleventh century also shaped the future boundaries of Europe. Crusade was inspired by a combination of the specific theology of good works developed by Latin Christians, problems with unruly knights, growing apocalypticism, and fears of military expansions of the Seljuk Turks into the eastern Mediterranean region.[11] In 1095, the Byzantine Emperor Alexius Comnenus asked Pope Urban II in Rome for assistance in recruiting troops to engage the Seljuks. After the schism of 1054, requesting help must have been a difficult decision for Alexius, who regarded the Germanic peoples to his west as uncouth barbarians. It might also seem surprising that Urban II agreed to help his rival. But Urban was driven by an apocalypticism that saw Seljuk military expansion as part of a holy war. "God exhorts you [bishops] as heralds of Christ," Urban is reported to have said, "to repeatedly urge men of all ranks whatsoever, knights as well as foot-soldiers, rich and poor, to hasten to exterminate this vile race [Muslims] from our lands and to aid the Christian inhabitants."[12] According to many estimates, about 150,000 Latin Christians responded to Urban's call to battle. The story of this First Crusade is extraordinary—it involves the march of tens of thousands (including women and children) over three thousand miles, as well as unplanned massacres of Jews, Christian violence against fellow Christians, sometimes surprising cooperation with Muslims, and all manners of deceit and plunder. It culminated with crusaders' capture of Jerusalem in 1099 and a gruesome slaughter of the city's inhabitants.[13] Overall, though, the First Crusade (and the crusades that followed) turned out to be a resounding failure. In the 1100s, the Kurdish Ayyubid leader Salah ad-Din (1137–1193) defeated the last crusaders in the eastern Mediterranean. By the 1300s the region was conquered by the Mamluks, a Turkic-speaking group of slaves who revolted against the Ayyubid dynasty. Ironically, the territory that Christians called the Holy Land (because it's where Jesus lived) ended up outside Christendom.

11. Christopher Tyerman, *Fighting for Christianity: Holy War and the Crusades* (Oxford: Oxford University Press, 2004).

12. Fulcher of Chartres, *A History of the Expedition to Jerusalem, 1095–1127*, trans. Frances Rita Ryan (Knoxville: University of Tennessee Press, 1969), 66.

13. Steven Runciman, *The First Crusade*, Canto ed. (Cambridge: Cambridge University Press, 1992).

One decision that proved critical in defining the boundaries of Christendom can be dated to 1469, when the princess Isabella of Castile secretly betrothed and married the prince of a neighboring kingdom, Ferdinand of Aragon, against the wishes of her half-bother, King Enrique IV. At the time, the peninsula of Iberia – where the two lived – had five kingdoms: Castile, Aragon, Navarre, Portugal, and the Emirate of Granada. When Enrique died in 1474, Isabella became queen of Castile and Ferdinand became king *jure uxoris* (Latin for "by right of his wife"). When Ferdinand's father died five years later, the crowns merged. Ferdinand and Isabella's combined kingdom—called Spain—became the most powerful state in Iberia, allowing them to intensify a crusade against Granada, ruled by Sultan Muhammad XII.[14] By 1492, after a long siege of Muhammad's fortified capital, Ferdinand's army forced the sultan to surrender. As a result of these events, the boundaries of Christendom expanded to the entire Iberian Peninsula.[15]

Another key military development that defined the geographical scope of Christendom was the fifteenth-century advances of the Ottoman Empire. The Ottomans were a Turkic people who began capturing lands in Asia Minor (present-day Turkey) in the thirteenth century. By 1453, the Ottomans—under Sultan Mehmed II—besieged and captured Constantinople, which the sultan renamed Istanbul. Constantine's Christian capital was gone, as was the last remnant of the Roman Empire. In later years, the Ottomans expanded into lands that today we would identify as southeastern Europe (present-day Greece, Bulgaria, and Romania, for instance).

By 1500, a set of historical developments—largely a combination of conversion efforts and military campaigns—led to a situation such that most of the lands that we today call Europe were governed by a variety of rulers—emperors, tsars, kings, dukes, counts, and otherwise—who shared a commitment to Christianity, and who tied allegiance to their faith and obedience to their political authority. The geographical boundaries of what would later become Europe were mostly set. Non-Christians in these lands—as historians of Judaism have shown all too well—were often seen as inherent threats to their Christian neighbors.[16]

---

14. For a Christian perspective on these crusades, see Joseph F. O'Callaghan, *Reconquest and Crusade in Medieval Spain* (Philadelphia: University of Pennsylvania Press, 2003). For a Muslim perspective, see L. P. Harvey, *Islamic Spain, 1250 to 1500* (Chicago: University of Chicago Press, 1990).

15. Ferdinand incorporated the Basque Kingdom of Navarre under his rule in 1512. The kingdom of Spain was only formally unified under Charles I, grandson of Ferdinand and Isabella, in 1516. In 1580, Charles's son Philip II captured Portugal. Spain held the entire Iberian Peninsula until 1640, when Portuguese merchants and nobles launched a successful rebellion.

16. León Poliakov, *The History of Anti-Semitism: Volume I: From the Time of Christ to the Court Jews* (New York: Vanguard Press, 1965).

The Collapse of Christendom and the Age of Religious Wars

Just about the time that the boundaries of Christendom were established, Christendom began to collapse. In the east, not only had Byzantium fallen to the Ottomans, but the disastrous reign of Tsar Ivan IV (called "the Terrible") left Russia in a state of comprehensive "political, social, institutional and moral collapse" in ways that profoundly crippled the country for over a century.[17] In the Latin West, a series of devastating wars broke out and over a million people came to be displaced as a result of the intolerant logic that Christians had inherited from the ancient and medieval worlds. The Reformation was the leading cause of Latin Christendom's collapse. You might have in your mind a triumphant picture of a monk named Martin Luther defiantly posting ninety-five theses to a church door in Wittenberg on October 31, 1517. Even if that event happened—and historians have long debated the question—neither Luther nor church leaders imagined schism as an option at the time. Only by 1520–1521 did it become clear that Latin Christendom itself was threatened.[18] Within a period of twelve months, Luther articulated a coherent rejection of church teaching, Pope Leo X excommunicated him, and powerful princes were providing him support. In some cases, alignment of political officials with the Protestant cause was the result of genuine conversion. In other cases, it was opportunism; kings, princes, nobles, and city magistrates merely took advantage of the internal theological disagreements to strengthen their position relative to competitors. Over the years, the ruptures became more defined, the polemic more vitriolic, and the efforts to reunite Latin Christendom more futile. Protestants lambasted Catholic worship as "vile filth" and decried the sexual delinquency of priests. Meanwhile, Catholics described Protestantism as "pollution" and claimed that Protestants used secret services as a pretext for orgies. Both sides described the other as "vermin" or an "infection."[19] Opposing sides thus presented dehumanized images of the other; they saw the chasm between one another as that between Christ and Satan. In locations across Christendom, ideological and social differences promoted constitutional crises and sometimes outright war.

The first religious war erupted between Protestant and Catholic territories in the Swiss lands from 1529 to 1531. In 1546 and again in 1552, the Holy Roman Empire, one of the inheritors of the former Germanic kingdoms in the region we now call Central Europe, broke into war between princes who supported Luther and those who backed the Catholic emperor.[20] France experienced

---

17. Robert O. Crummey, *The Formation of Moscovy, 1304–1613* (London: Longman, 1987), 205.

18. For a recent treatment, see Lyndal Roper, *Martin Luther: Renegade and Prophet* (New York: Random House, 2017).

19. See Natalie Zemon Davis, "The Rites of Violence," *Past & Present*, 59 (1973): 51–91.

20. Joachim Whaley, *Germany and the Holy Roman Empire*, vol. 1 (Oxford: Oxford University Press, 2012), 304–36.

a devastating eight wars from 1562 to 1598 largely between the Catholic govern-ment and Protestants (funded by wealthy nobles and merchants) who wanted to protect their faith, but also their autonomy from royal coercion.[21] Sometimes these wars were marked not just by battlefield bloodshed, but by popular vio-lence, including some shocking massacres, most stunningly one in Paris in 1572 in which Catholics slaughtered over two thousand Protestants in the streets in a matter of days. The Netherlands experienced civil war from 1566 to 1648.[22] Protestants allied with nobles and urban magistrates who opposed Catholic royal centralization. Widespread religious violence broke out in 1566–1567, including Protestant attacks on churches and monasteries that ignited three generations of warfare.[23] That war later became intertwined with the Thirty Years' War (1618–1648). Hostilities began with a local skirmish in Prague, but ultimately included nearly all of Europe's leading powers and left many regions decimated on an un-precedented scale. Protracted sieges of heavily fortified cities caused massive death tolls, directly through warfare, but also through depleted harvests and plague outbreaks made possible by horrible living conditions. Fifteen to twenty percent of Europe's population died as a result of the Thirty Years' War. In some regions, populations declined by more than two-thirds. While describing the Thirty Years' War as a religious war risks underemphasizing its secular causes, there is no doubt that this devastating set of conflicts drew on political and religious ten-sions ignited by the Reformation.[24] The same could be said about England's Civil War (1642–1651), which likewise brought widespread bloodshed.[25]

The religious wars drew on the same logic of intolerance that Latin Christians inherited from Christian Rome: allegiance to the church was required for mem-bership in most political, cultural, and economic systems. Most people—though certainly not all—viewed anyone who did not belong to their church as an inher-ent threat. In 1567, after the iconoclastic riots in the Netherlands, the government oversaw perhaps the most sudden, intense, and complete suppression of dissent of this era. Tens of thousands of Protestants were convicted of heresy and rebellion. Most were never caught, but were convicted in absentia. Dissenters flooded into exile in the Holy Roman Empire and England. Many French Protestants also fled

---

21. Mack P. Holt, *The French Wars of Religion, 1562–1629*, 2nd ed. (Cambridge: Cambridge University Press, 2005).

22. Geoffrey Parker, *The Dutch Revolt* (Ithaca, NY: Cornell University Press, 1977).

23. Peter J. Arnade, *Beggars, Iconoclasts, and Civic Patriots: The Political Culture of the Dutch Revolt* (Ithaca, NY: Cornell University Press, 2008).

24. Peter H. Wilson, *The Thirty Years War: Europe's Tragedy* (Cambridge, MA: Belknap Press, 2009).

25. John Morrill, "The Religious Context of the English Civil War," *Transactions of the Royal Historical Society* 34 (1984): 155–78. Charles W. A. Prior and Glenn Burgess, eds., *England's Wars of Religion, Revisited* (Farnham, UK: Ashgate, 2011).

persecution for cities in the Holy Roman Empire (like Strasbourg) or the Swiss Confederation (like Geneva). Netherlandish and French refugees printed clandestine books for smuggling back into their home countries. They also plotted their revenge. When the French religious wars finally ended in 1598, Protestants were legally allowed to live in France, but the effort to expel "heretics" never disappeared from the minds of some Catholics. By 1685, King Louis XIV decided that he had enough power to make this dream a reality. He revoked the law legalizing Protestantism in France. Over 150,000 Protestants went into exile in the Dutch Republic, England, and elsewhere.[26]

We should not get the idea that it was Catholics doing all the expelling and Protestants always the victims. Every time Protestants gained the upper hand, forced migrations of Catholics followed. When Protestant rebels captured the northern territories of the Netherlands, Catholics fled to the Holy Roman Empire and the Southern Netherlands.[27] In England, when the Protestant Queen Elizabeth came to power in 1558 after the death of her Catholic sister, many Catholics fled. English Catholic communities popped up in the Southern Netherlands, France, the Italian peninsula, and Spain. Wealthy English Catholics also established convents and schools in Catholic territories on the continent, so that their children could be educated in their faith rather than in the Protestant schools back home.[28] Catholic refugees also printed books for smuggling back home and conspired against the government.

Non-Christians were the subjects of expulsions during this era as well. Even before the Reformation, following their victory over the Emirate of Granada in 1492, Ferdinand and Isabella expelled all Jews from Spain, to complete their efforts to create a purified Christian kingdom. The Spanish Inquisition treated Jews who stayed as de facto Christians—they were called *conversos*—and punished anyone who practiced Judaism. Within the first four months after the expulsion, 35,000–40,000 Jews went into exile.[29] Many moved to Portugal, hoping that the expulsion order was only temporary. Not only were they wrong, but the king of

26. Susanne Lachenicht, *Hugenotten in Europa und Nordamerika: Migration und Integration in der Frühen Neuzeit* (Frankfurt: Campus Verlag, 2010).

27. Geert H. Janssen, *The Dutch Revolt and Catholic Exile in Reformation Europe* (Cambridge: Cambridge University Press, 2014).

28. See, for instance, Liesbeth Corens, "Saints Beyond Borders: Relics and the Expatriate English Catholic Community," in *Exile and Religious Identity, 1500–1800*, ed. Jesse Spohnholz and Gary K. Waite (London: Routledge, 2018), 25–38. Cano-Echavarría and Ana Sáez-Hidalgo, "Educating for Martyrdom: British Exiles in the English College at Valladolid," in *Religious Diaspora in Early Modern Europe*, ed. Timothy G. Fehler, Greta Grace Kroeker, Charles H. Parker, and Jonathan Ray (London: Pickering & Chatto, 2014), 93–106.

29. Henry Kamen, *The Spanish Inquisition: A Historical Revision* (New Haven, CT: Yale University Press, 1998), 18–27.

Portugal followed with an expulsion order in 1497 and thousands had to flee that country as well. Elsewhere in Europe, with a rigorous Catholic Reformation, anti-Jewish purges ramped up in the mid-sixteenth century. When Protestants took over territories, they were no less hostile to Jews. There were waves of expulsions of Jews from Protestant territories of the Holy Roman Empire through the 1540s and 1550s. Christians of all types often told absurd stories of Jews scheming against Christians, poisoning wells, and—most shockingly—ritually murdering Christian infants, whose blood they supposedly needed for their satanic rituals.[30] Driven by these fantasies, the historian Jonathan Israel has argued that by the 1570s anti-Jewish Christians had managed to achieve to "the near-elimination of Jewish life from western and central Europe."[31]

These expulsions targeted Muslims too. After 1492, some 200,000 Muslims still lived under Spanish rule. In many places, they were the majority of the population, so complete suppression was impossible. But that doesn't mean that Spain's rulers didn't try.[32] From 1499, Christians violently coerced Muslims to accept baptisms, seized mosques and converted them into churches, and suppressed Muslim religious texts, halal foods, and the practice of circumcision. These efforts sparked rebellions, which only further stoked fears among Christians. Often Christians feared that Muslims in Spain would become a kind of fifth column that worked to undermined Christendom from within, even as they feared that Ottoman Turks would undermine it from without in kind of anti-Christian crusade.[33] Thus, in Castile in 1502 and Aragon in 1525, Muslims were given the choice to convert or leave. By 1526, any Muslim who remained in Spain was considered to have converted—and called a *morisco*. Further tensions exploded in a massive revolt in 1568. By 1609 fears of further rebellions and the failure to suppress Islam encouraged the Spanish king to order the expulsion of all people of Muslim dissent. An estimated 300,000 moriscos fled, as depicted in Figure 1.1.

How did people respond to these forced dislocations? There is no single answer. Some hosts were driven by compassion and mercy for refugees, while others viewed the newcomers with suspicion and fear. Complaints emerged across Europe that refugees drove up rent and food prices. There was sometimes

---

30. R. Po. Chia Hsia, *The Myth of Ritual Murder: Jews and Magic in Reformation Germany* (New Haven. CT: Yale University Press, 1988).

31. Jonathan I. Israel, *European Jewry in the Age of Mercantilism*, 3rd ed. (Portland, OR: The Littman Library, 1998), 4.

32. The following summarizes from Matthew Carr, *Blood and Faith: The Purging of Muslim Spain* (New York: The New Press, 2009).

33. Paula S. Fichtner, *Terror and Toleration: The Habsburg Empire Confronts Islam, 1526–1850* (London: Reaktion Books, 2008).

FIGURE 1.1 Muslims fleeing Catholic Spain. From Georg Braun and Frans Hogenberg, *Civitates Orbis Terrarum* (Cologne: Peter von Brachen, 1616, orig. 1572). *Source*: Library of Congress

not enough housing for the newcomers, who had to sleep on the streets or camp just outside city gates. Foreigners drained supplies of grain and clothing. The most desperate refugees were reduced to stealing. Many locals treated the refugees as dangers to the state, community, and social order. They painted refugees as religious zealots—the most extreme and uncompromising kind of people who rejected local customs. An example of this comes from a Dutch politician, Nicolaas van der Laan, who portrayed refugees as extremists who threatened peace.[34] It turns out, however, that some of Van der Laan's closest friends and relatives were religious refugees. It seems clear that he only used this rhetoric to discredit his political opponents. This kind of xenophobic stereotyping was common in the Holy Roman Empire, England, the Italian peninsula, and elsewhere.

Hostility to refugees came from those who saw them not just as religious threats but economic threats. New regulations restricted exiles' economic activities. In places that hosted refugees, governments made stiffer rules for starting a trade, limitations on how many foreigners could work in a particular business, and demanded special fees levied from foreign workers. One example from England in 1589 comes from the weavers' guild, which ordered that a master could only have one journeyman in his shop who came from the Dutch and French refugees. Any foreign weaver was limited to owning only three looms, while local weavers could have as many as they could afford.[35] Geneva in the 1540s also put similar restrictions on the work of French refugees.[36] Rules like this proliferated. So

---

34. Johannes Müller, *Exile Memories and the Dutch Revolt: The Narrated Diaspora, 1550–1750* (Leiden: Brill, 2016), 103–07.

35. Scott Oldenburg, *Alien Albion: Literature and Immigration in Early Modern England* (Toronto: University of Toronto Press, 2014), 83.

36. William G. Naphy, *Calvin and the Consolidation of the Genevan Reformation* (Manchester: Manchester University Press, 1994), 122–25.

too did anti-immigrant petitions, such as one presented by citizens of London in 1571, complaining about foreigners who refused to follow local commerce laws.[37] In the Holy Roman Empire we also see grievances against refugees, for instance the complaint in the city of Wesel in 1580 that bakers who had fled from the Netherlands introduced unfair competition to the local bread makers. One local complained that "all the strangers were thieves."[38]

Many hosts didn't want charity to go to refugees instead of needy locals. New restrictions were put on social welfare institutions—including poor houses, hospitals, and orphanages—requiring that only locals could receive help. Yet desperate and impoverished refugees usually lacked networks of family and friends who might otherwise help them. In Geneva, the church established the *Bourse française*, an institution separate from civic social welfare institutions, which supported the poor and needy among the refugees from France.[39] Similar kinds of formal and informal institutions were established elsewhere as well. Men sometimes asked women to orchestrate and coordinate care for the refugees—tasks that had largely fallen to men in previous years—because there simply was too much work to do.[40]

There were sympathetic voices who defended refugees as well. Some businessmen and politicians appreciated their contributions to the local economy. Some clergymen were moved by compassion and mercy. But all across the former lands of Christendom refugees faced xenophobia, stereotyping, and fears that they might undermine the local economic, political, and social structures. In the long run, though, the doomsayers and fearmongers proved unable to predict the future. By and large, the refugees did not turn out to be religious zealots bent on transforming their host societies to fit their worldview. Many proved to be peaceful neighbors, willing to compromise when asked and most interested in establishing a stable life for themselves and fitting into their new society. Jewish immigrants from Spain coming to the Italian peninsula learned Italian, participated peacefully in local trade with Catholics, and kept displays of their Judaism that might be deemed strange or threatening out of public sight.[41] The same was

---

37. Andrew Pettegree, *Foreign Protestant Communities in Sixteenth-Century London* (Oxford: Clarendon Press, 1986), 282.

38. Jesse Spohnholz, *The Tactics of Toleration: A Refugee Community in the Age of Religious Wars* (Newark: University of Delaware Press, 2011), 194.

39. Jeannine E. Olson, *Calvin and Social Welfare: Deacons and the Bourse française* (Selinsgrove, PA: Susquehanna University Press, 1989).

40. Jesse Spohnholz, "Olympias and Chrysostem: The Debate over Wesel's Reformed Deaconesses, 1568–1609," *Archiv für Reformationsgeschichte* 98 (2007): 84–106.

41. Kenneth Stow, *Theater of Acculturation: The Roman Ghetto in the 16th Century* (Seattle: University of Washington Press, 2001).

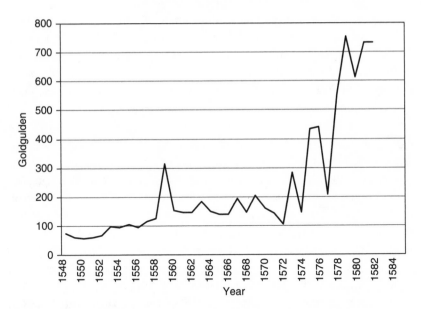

FIGURE 1.2 Loading Crane Incomes in Wesel, 1548–1585, in gold guilders.

often true with the French and Dutch refugees in England and the Holy Roman Empire.[42] Within a generation, tempers usually cooled, as a younger cohort of hosts and refugees born abroad came to see the arrangements as normal.

Sometimes, refugees brought economic and technological innovations that proved a great boon to the local economy.[43] When Protestant weavers from the Netherlands fled to England and the Holy Roman Empire, they taught local weavers to make fancy silks and laces that were sought after by wealthy Renaissance elites. Production of these "new draperies" inspired the construction of factories, required hiring new apprentices, and spurred international trade. Take a look at Figure 1.2, for instance, which comes from my archival research into the Dutch refugees living in Wesel, a medium-sized town in the Holy Roman Empire. It shows incomes from the city's loading crane. Merchants paid a fee to the city, which operated the crane, to move crates of goods onto ships for transport. The rise in incomes you see corresponds to the arrival of waves of refugees. In this case, the government richly benefited from welcoming the foreigners.

---

42. Andrew Spicer, "A Process of Gradual Assimilation: The Exile Community in Southampton, 1567–1635," *Proceedings of the Huguenot Society* 26 (1995): 186–98. Spohnholz, *Tactics of Toleration*.

43. L. B. Luu, *Immigrants and the Industries of London, 1500–1700* (Aldershot, UK: Ashgate, 2005).

Foreign merchants fleeing persecution brought their business with them, but also maintained trade ties back home. The Van der Meulen family is a good example. Forced to flee certain persecution in the Southern Netherlands (a territory roughly where Belgium is today), the Van der Meulens moved to cities across Europe and brought with them their enormous trade connections that had made them fabulously wealthy back in Antwerp.[44] Some of their relatives stayed behind as loyal Catholics, but maintained business relationships and family bonds with their Protestant relatives in exile. Daniel van der Meulen moved first to Bremen, while his sister Sara and her husband fled to Cologne, and his brother-in-law Jacques moved to London. Wherever they went, they brought the family's trade in Italian silks, Spanish wines, and Portuguese spices. They also accessed new markets. Bremen offered Daniel van der Meulen access to Baltic grain and fish markets, for instance. Historians like Clé Lesger have argued that the experience of fleeing to foreign lands actually benefited merchants, since cosmopolitanism and international relationships were so important for the profession.[45] The idea is tempting. But recently Jesse Sadler has cautioned that there were too many hurdles to trading in foreign lands to think that merchants in exile were anywhere close to *more successful* than those who were left unhindered to operate their businesses back home. Merchants who fled as refugees often lacked contacts and reputations so critical for traders, and transportation and communication links during times of war and persecution could be risky. Yet Lesger is correct that when wealthy merchants fled persecution for other cities, they could transform economies. When he moved to the Dutch Republic, Daniel van der Meulen played a role in that country's meteoritic rise to global trade hegemony, as well as the economic collapse of his former home of Antwerp.

The same is true for Jewish refugees. One notable example is Jews' role as moneylenders. Because of medieval prohibitions against moneylending for Christians, some Jewish bankers and merchants came to specialize in this occupation—effectively operating as lending banks to governments and businessmen alike. The mass expulsions of Jews from Spain and Portugal brought these skills to the Ottoman Empire, Italian lands, the Dutch Republic, and the Holy Roman Empire. Jewish moneylenders helped governments deal with debts, invested in large business ventures, and helped resource military operations.[46] The Dutch East India Company, the first joint stock company in world history, had substantial financial backing from Jewish merchants and bankers who had moved to the Dutch Republic as refugees. My point here is not to argue that accepting

---

44. J. R. Sadler, "Family in Revolt: The Van der Meulen and Della Faille Families in the Dutch Revolt" (PhD diss., UCLA, 2015).

45. Clé Lesger, *The Rise of the Amsterdam Market and Information Exchange* (Aldershot, UK: Ashate, 2006), 166.

46. Israel, *European Jewry*, 101–18.

refugees was always an economically lucrative decision. It would be both overly simplistic and probably impossible to tally up the financial costs and benefits to welcoming refugees. There are simply too many factors to calculate and, especially for these early refugee crises, too few surviving sources to come up with accurate numbers. Even if we could do so, there would be no way of comparing our results to the economic impacts of an alternative reality with no refugees. Rather, my central point is that the rhetoric of xenophobia that emphasized the financial toll that refugees would inflict showed very little clairvoyance in the short or long term.

There were all sorts of other impacts that refugees brought to their host societies. They introduced new ways of communicating, new clothing styles, and new religious ideas, for instance. Consider the example of artists. During the bleak days of persecution, famed painters from the Flemish Renaissance who had embraced Protestantism moved to England and the Holy Roman Empire. In Cologne, London, and Frankfurt, groups of artists emerged from the 1560s who brought Renaissance artistic styles with them. Jan de Critz, for instance, escaped the Netherlands, later becoming painter to the king of England.[47] Gillis van Coninxloo, the Flemish landscape painter, fled first up the Rhine River to a town in the Holy Roman Empire and them to Amsterdam, where he became part of the famed Dutch Golden Age of painting.[48]

The two states that were probably the most impacted from the arrival of floods of refugees in the post-Reformation era were the Ottoman Empire and the Dutch Republic. Both states showed a high degree of flexibility and porousness of religious, political, and ethnic boundaries relative to neighboring states, which made them more amenable to integrating foreigners of different faiths. In the case of the Ottoman Empire, the fact that nomadic and transient lives were common made the integration of refugees easier.[49] The Ottoman Turks' brand of Sunni Islam was also not existentially threatened by the existence of alternate religions in the way that many Christian worldviews were. While many religious minorities chose to convert to Islam under Ottoman rule, Christians and Jews were permitted to worship freely and maintain a high degree of autonomy if they wanted. This was in part a result of how most Muslims understood Sharia's attitude toward *dhimmi*, or People of the Book. This legal distinction originally applied to non-Muslims who

47. Karen Hearn, "Insiders or Outsiders? Overseas-born Artists at the Jacobean Court," in *From Strangers to Citizens: The Integration of Immigrant Communities in Britain, Ireland and Colonial America, 1550–1750*, ed. Richard Vigne and Charles Littleton (Portland, OR: Sussex Academic Press, 2001), 117–26.

48. Heinrich Gerhard Franz, "Der Landschaftmaler Gillis van Coninxloo," in *Kunst, Kommerz, Glaubenskampf: Frankenthal um 1600*, ed. Edgar Hürkey (Worms: Wernersche Verlagsgesellschaft, 1995), 103–13.

49. Reşat Kasaba, *A Moveable Empire: Ottoman Nomads, Migrants, and Refugees* (Seattle: University of Washington Press, 2009).

were also part of the Abrahamic scriptural tradition (thus, Jews and Christians), but was also variously applied to all sorts of non-Muslims living under Muslim governments. In the Ottoman Empire, dhimmi were permitted religious freedom and granted extensive judicial and social autonomy provided they paid a special tax. In Ottoman cities, Christians, Muslims, and Jews mixed peacefully on the streets and in bustling markets. Istanbul became a lively polylingual, polyethnic, and polyreligious metropolis—more so than any city in the former lands of Latin Christendom. While historians used to portray Ottoman treatment of religious minorities as part of a coordinated policy, recent scholarship has shown that it was ad hoc, diverse, and flexible.[50] There were rules about wearing distinctive clothing to ensure that religious minorities displayed their second-class legal status and prohibitions on building new churches and synagogues, but these orders were often not enforced. Many Christians and Jews also preferred to settle cases in Sharia courts rather than those run by their coreligionists.

Ottomans rulers even actively courted refugees to help repopulate dilapidated former Byzantine lands now under their control. Among the conversos fleeing the Spanish and Portuguese expulsions described earlier, the largest number went to the Ottoman Empire. The city of Salonika (present-day Thessaloniki, in Greece) provides a remarkable example. At the time of the expulsion of Jews from Spain in 1492, most Jews had left the city, unhappy with Ottoman rule. By 1519— only one generation later—Iberian Jews came to make up more than half of the city's population and had built twenty-four synagogues.[51] The Mendes family, converso merchants who moved to Istanbul, became among the wealthiest and most powerful families in the empire.[52] Iberian Jews brought with them to the Ottoman lands skills and capital as merchants, bankers, interpreters, diplomats, and doctors.[53] Some Christians too who had run afoul of Catholic authorities— because they rejected the doctrine of the Trinity or the church's teachings on good works, for example—fled to the Ottoman Empire as well.[54]

The Ottoman Empire was also a favorite refuge for Muslims fleeing expulsion from Spain. They too brought new trades with them. The historian Suraiya

50. Benjamin Braude, "Foundational Myths of the *Millet* System," in *Christians & Jews in the Ottoman Empire*, ed. Benjamin Braude (Boulder, CO: Lynne Rienner, 2014), 65–85.

51. Daniel Goffman, *The Ottoman Empire and Early Modern Europe* (Cambridge: Cambrdge University Press, 2002), 87–88, 177.

52. Halil Inalcik, "Capital Formation in the Ottoman Empire," *Journal of Economic History* 29, no. 1 (1969): 121–22.

53. Minna Rozen, *A History of the Jewish Community in Istanbul: The Formative Years, 1453– 1566* (Leiden: Brill, 2002), 228–43.

54. Suraiya Faroqui, *Travel and Artisans in the Ottoman Empire: Employment and Mobility in the Early Modern Era* (New York: I. B. Tauris, 2014), 51.

Faroqhi offers the example of the production of a kind of brimless hat called a *chechia* that became popular all around the Mediterranean (and remains popular today in Tunisia).[55] It was not just Muslims fleeing Christian-ruled lands who fled to the Ottoman Empire. When the Safavid dynasty took over in present-day Iran, Sunni Muslims fled to Ottoman lands in large numbers. Previously, Sunni Muslims had dominated Iran and the Safavids were only a mystical religious order with Twelver Shi'ite ideology—a belief system that awaits a future twelfth "hidden" imam called the Mahdi who will usher in a new age of peace and justice. After the collapse of the Timurid Empire, in 1501 the hereditary Grand Master of the Safavid order, Ismail, consolidated the region under his control as shah. He established Shi'ism as the new state religion and claimed an absolutist and divinely mandated role as representative of the Mahdi on earth.[56] Fearing persecution, many Sunnis fled Safavid rule. In the Ottoman Empire, educated Sunni Persian refugees became sought after for their familiarity with Farsi literature.[57]

Almost as soon as it was established in the 1570s, the Dutch Republic also started attracting religious refugees. The new state officially maintained most of the same intolerant logic that prevailed elsewhere in the former lands of Christendom. Yet because members of the state-sponsored Protestant church made up only about 10 percent of the population, it was unrealistic to enforce intolerance. The result was a decentralized republic that became the most religiously diverse in the lands that once made up Christendom, largely a result of informal, off-the-record compromises. Religious minorities worshiped in barely concealed house churches, which were a kind of public secret across the republic.[58] As with the Ottoman Empire, large numbers of refugees fleeing to the Dutch Republic were coreligionists facing hardship elsewhere. Thus, Calvinists from French-speaking parts of the Southern Netherlands found refuge in Dutch cities like Amsterdam, Haarlem, and Leiden. After 1685, about fifty thousand French Calvinists, called Huguenots, fled persecution for the Dutch Republic, where they joined the French-speaking churches established by refugees a century earlier.[59] As the Dutch Republic's financial fortunes soared and it developed a

55. Faroqui, *Travel and Artisans*, 47.

56. Roger Savory, *Iran Under the Safavids* (Cambridge: Cambridge University Press, 1980), 27–49.

57. Faroqui, *Travel and Artisans*, 47–48.

58. Benjamin J. Kaplan, "Fictions of Privacy: House Chapels and the Spatial Accommodation of Religious Dissent in Early Modern Europe," *American Historical Review* 107, no. 4 (2002): 1031–64.

59. David van der Linden, *Experiencing Exile: Huguenot Refugees in the Dutch Republic, 1680–1700* (Farnham, UK: Ashgate, 2014).

FIGURE 1.3 Interior of Esnoga. Painting by Emanuel de Witte, 1680.
Source: Rijksmuseum

reputation for religious pluralism, migrants of other faiths started arriving as well, especially in the new commercial metropolis of Amsterdam.

Jewish refugees fleeing Spain started moving to the Dutch Republic in the 1590s.[60] Soon after, the Beth Jacob congregation was organized in Amsterdam, followed by Neve Shalom and Beth Israel. By 1639, the three congregations combined and built their first public synagogue. Thirty years later they built an even grander one—called Esnoga, pictured in Figure 1.3.[61] Their *mahamad* (governing board) functioned openly and the congregation printed Jewish devotional works freely. Esnoga became a famed attraction. Foreign visitors to the city like John Evelyn and William Brereton described seeing the synagogue's holy ark (where Torah scrolls were kept). Visitors became so numerous that they were disturbing worship. The answer of the congregation was not to exclude Christians from their building, but to put up a boundary from which the visitors could watch real-life

---

60. Miriam Bodian, *Hebrews of the Portuguese Naion: Conversos and Community in Early Modern Amsterdam* (Bloomington: Indiana University Press, 1997).

61. Steven Nadler, *Rembrandt's Jews* (Chicago: University of Chicago Press, 2003).

Judaism being practiced. Records report that congregants often walked over to the visitors to greet the gentiles personally. For those who stopped in, Judaism may have appeared strange, but it also looked pretty mundane. After all, visitors did not witness Jews plotting with Satan or killing Christian babies for magical practices—stereotypes of Judaism that had long filled Christian imaginations—but instead ordinary people engaged in nonthreatening religious devotion.

The Creation of Europe

Even generations after Christendom's collapse, it remained common to treat Europe and Christendom as synonyms.[62] But by the late 1600s, Europe had come to mean something wholly different—it was now a collection of states that shared a set of diplomatic ties, political forms, and, as we'll see elsewhere in this book, a chauvinistic attitude toward people from elsewhere in the world. Two key steps in this transformation included two interrelated changes, one practical and financial—the emergence of large bureaucratic states as normative—and other in terms of worldviews—the idea that these states shared a secular foundation (we will cover a critical third step, colonialism, in chapter 2).

Seen from within Europe, the religious divisions created by the Reformation played a critical role in promoting warfare, and that warfare played a critical role in expanding the bureaucratic systems that became the basis of European politics. In his 1972 study, the historian Geoffrey Parker used the logistics of the Spanish military to show the interrelationships between state finances, bureaucracies, warfare, and political survival during this period.[63] Armies needed to grow larger, to enable long-term sieges required to defeat new fortifications capable of withstanding cannon fire. At the start of the sixteenth century, large campaigns required 20,000 troops. By the end of the century, they took over 100,000. The coordination required to recruit, train, pay, and discipline armies skyrocketed too. It was not just soldiers and their commanders who moved across the countryside. Women (including wives, companions, and servants) did laundry and cooked for armies. Other men purchased and distributed clothes and food. A medical staff was needed as well. Shops and brothels grew up around the camps. In a way, these were not just armies, but travelling cities. Another reason that military campaigns became more expensive was the emergence of navies. Building ships was enormously expensive and sailors needed superior training to army soldiers. The most stunning example was the Spanish

---

62. Hay, *Europe*, 109–10.

63. Geoffrey Parker, *The Army of Flanders and the Spanish Road, 1567–1659*, 2nd ed. (Cambridge: Cambridge University Press, 2004).

Armada, which was made up of about 125 ships carrying over 2,500 cannons and 30,000 sailors and soldiers.[64]

Each state needed to increase its ability to raise funds if it was going to succeed in war. One way to increase revenues was to request permission for new taxes from representative assemblies (usually made up of nobles and wealthy merchants). In order to get approval for new revenues to pay for her growing military, Queen Elizabeth I (r. 1558–1603) of England sought parliamentary approval over and over again, and each time she had to make another concession to Parliament.[65] Another way monarchs raised funds to pay for war was to sell royal offices. One study found that roughly 20 percent of costs of financing a French royal army in Orleans in 1570—over 76,000 livres—were borne by selling offices.[66] The price tag for these offices was steep: the cost of purchasing a position as councilor in the Paris law court was 6,000 livres in 1522; by 1600, the same post cost 60,000 livres![67] Another tactic to raise funds was the reliance on loans—sometimes even forced loans that merchants or nobles had no interest in supplying. The Spanish government relied heavily on short-term loans from bankers in Madrid, Antwerp, and Genoa.[68] In 1602, for example, the Genoese Centurione family of bankers loaned King Philip III nearly nineteen million florins to cover the cost of war. Governments who successfully managed precarious budgets were able to support large militaries both to defeat internal dissent and to swallow smaller states.[69]

The breakup of Christendom posed not only political and financial challenges, but also encouraged some to rethink the intolerant logic of Christendom by the late seventeenth century. The most important early center for this intellectual shift was the Dutch Republic, which was being transformed by waves of refugees and migrants of the post–Reformation era. We can see this through three men—Baruch Spinoza, John Locke, and Pierre Bayle—who all had deep personal ties to the era's refugee crises and became advocates of religious toleration.[70] Spinoza came from

---

64. Colin Martin and Geoffrey Parker, *The Spanish Armada*, rev. ed. (New York: Mandolin, 1999).

65. Wallace MacCaffrey, *Elizabeth I: War and Politics, 1588–1603* (Princeton, NJ: Princeton University Press, 1992), 59–69.

66. James B. Wood, *The King's Army: Warfare, Soldiers, and Society during the Wars of Religion in France, 1562–1576* (Cambridge: Cambridge University Press, 1996), 292.

67. Merry Wiesner-Hanks, *Early Modern Europe, 1450–1789*, 2nd ed. (Cambridge: Cambridge University Press, 2013), 105.

68. Parker, *Army of Flanders*, 123–31.

69. Mark Greengrass, *Christendom Destroyed: Europe, 1517–1648* (New York: Penguin, 2014), 262–69.

70. Perez Zagorin, *How the Idea of Religious Toleration Came to the West* (Princeton, NJ: Princeton University Press, 2003).

Amsterdam's community of Jews who arrived as refugees from Iberia. In 1671 he argued that religious truths were largely unknowable and that religious texts simply could not be read literally.[71] While Spinoza's target was rabbinic authority and the Hebrew Bible, many Christians grew concerned that his arguments also undermined their religion and its promise of eternal salvation. From Spinoza's perspective, persecution and religious war looked senseless, while toleration looked rational. Locke was an anti-Trinitarian dissenter from England who fled to the Dutch Republic. In his 1689 *Letter on Toleration*, he argued that political authorities did not have the ability to punish matters of conscience or coerce church attendance. Government exists, he wrote, to protect "Life, Liberty, Health and Indolency of Body and Possession of Property," not to ensure salvation. Nor can any person "abandon the care of his own Salvation, as blindly to leave it to the choice of any other, whether Prince or Subject, to prescribe to him what Faith or Worship he shall embrace."[72] Bayle was a French Protestant refugee who had fled his country after Louis XIV banned his faith in 1685. In 1697 he argued that force and coercion can never be the outcome of true faith, as Augustine had once argued, but are opposed to the basic principles of it. Toleration thus did not breed disunity and social collapse—as the older logic of Christendom maintained—but was instead the only way of maintaining peace in a world where differences of belief are inevitable.[73]

Well into the Enlightenment, of course, many viewed the toleration of religious minorities as the begrudging endurance of something dangerous or wrong.[74] They understood tolerance in a similar way that we talk of one's alcohol tolerance, that is, we mean how much of a bodily poison one can take before getting sick. My point in invoking Bayle, Locke, or Spinoza is not to suggest that their answers were the right ones or that they were heroes to the emulated. Rather, my point is this: all three lived in a world profoundly shaped by refugee crises. They saw evidence of this all around them. Jews, Huguenots, Socinians, Lutherans, Presbyterians, Mennonites, and Jews—refugees of all kinds—made the Dutch Republic their home. Their answers were not faultless by any means: after all "tolerance" can easily become a tool of exclusion and marginalization of second-class citizens. However, following the collapse of Christendom, people living in this part of the world did start seeing alternatives to the centuries-old intolerant logic of Christendom.

---

71. Benedictus de Spinoza, *Theological-Political Treatise*, ed. Jonathan Israel (Cambridge: Cambridge University Press, 2007).

72. John Locke, *A Letter on Toleration* (Indianapolis: Hackett, 1983), 26.

73. Pierre Bayle, *Political Writings*, ed. Sally Jenkinson (Cambridge: Cambridge University Press, 2000).

74. See, for instance, Benjamin J. Kaplan, *Cunegonde's Kidnapping: A Story of Religious Conflict in the Age of Enlightenment* (New Haven, CT: Yale University Press, 2014).

As Christendom fell apart, in its place, people started referring to this region as a *body of states* that were culturally united as Europe. Europe stopped being a synonym for Christendom. Instead it came to be used for the places that were left in Christendom's wake. In the new logic—the logic of Europe—political order did not depend on institutional promises of religious conformity to any state church. No longer were people living in this peninsula of Asia primarily bound together by their faith. Rightly or wrongly, they believed that they were bound together by a shared religious past, but also a shared present in which they could cooperate beyond religion. They were becoming European.

Conclusion

By the 1700s, the idea of Europe had become standard. It was a group of secular states bound by diplomatic ties, whose members imagined they shared a common history, and, as we will see in chapter 2, whose governments often shared the common experience overseeing colonial conquest in places around the world. Christendom's dream of a universal empire had collapsed. In the new way of thinking, each state in Europe expected to maintain its own sovereignty within Europe, even as many of them also claimed the right to conquer lands and peoples outside of Europe. Thus, by 1756, when Jean-Jacques Rousseau accurately described Europe as a descendant of the medieval idea of Christendom, he did so in order to propose a European Parliament, which might provide a secular, legal, and peaceful way to resolve disputes into the future. By revealing Europe's debt to Christendom, Rousseau explicitly suggested that Europeans had moved beyond their medieval past. But implicitly, he also acknowledged that Europe was not a continent but only a relatively recent idea.

Through the eighteenth century, however, the place of the Ottoman Empire relative to the new idea of Europe remained ambiguous. On the one hand, the empire remained an important part of eighteenth-century European politics. Diplomatically and economically, Ottomans participated actively in the European community. The Ottoman state also developed many of the same bureaucratic systems of warfare that made survival and expansion possible. On the other hand, Europeans continued to see Ottomans as outsiders. During the days of Christendom, Christians portrayed Turks as barbarous and cruel criminals consumed by bloodlust. Now, those images were replaced by equally unrealistic images of Turks as hapless fools incapable of the higher thinking of Europeans.[75] That's what Rousseau referred to when he wrote, in the quote that started this chapter, "that the one nation [in Europe] which had refused to accept Christianity

75. Fichtner, *Terror and Toleration*.

has always remained an alien among the rest." He meant that he believed that because the shared history of Christendom bound Europeans together, Turks would never be fully a part.[76] That is, while many Europeans valued Europe as secular, many continued to use their shared historical legacy of Christendom to provide legitimization for anti-Jewish and anti-Muslim sentiments and policies. In this way, the new metageography underpinning the idea of Europe could be both inclusive and exclusive, both peaceful and coercive, depending on one's position in the hierarchies of power. In chapter 2, we'll also see that the invention of Europe was part of the simultaneous invention of another metageography, the idea of America, which inspired other forms of refugee crises.

FURTHER READING

Greengrass, Mark. *Christendom Destroyed: Europe, 1517–1648*. New York: Penguin, 2014.

Kaplan, Benjamin. "The Legal Rights of Religious Refugees in the 'Refugee-Cities' of Early Modern Germany." *Journal of Refugee Studies* 32, no. 1 (2019): 86–105.

Kasaba, Reşat. *A Moveable Empire: Ottoman Nomads, Migrants & Refugees*. Seattle: University of Washington Press, 2009.

Spohnholz, Jesse, and Gary K. Waite, eds. *Exile and Religious Identity, 1500–1800*. London: Routledge, 2018.

Terpstra, Nicholas. *Religious Refugees in the Early Modern World: An Alternative History of the Reformation*. Cambridge: Cambridge University Press, 2015.

van der Linden, David. *Experiencing Exile: Huguenot Refugees in the Dutch Republic, 1680–1700*. Farnham, UK: Ashgate, 2014.

---

76. Rousseau made the Ottoman's exclusion from Europe explicit elsewhere. Rousseau, *A Lasting Peace*, 58, 66–67, 83.

2 COLONIALISM, REFUGEES, AND THE INVENTION OF AMERICA

N ot long after the idea of Europe had become stable in its present-day form—soon after Jean-Jacques Rousseau defined Europe as an inheritor of a now-dead Christendom—we find the first comprehensive English-language history of the America. In 1777, William Robertson, a Scottish preacher, published his *History of America*. In his preface, he wrote,

> The two volumes which I now publish, contain an account of the discovery of the New World, and of the progress of . . . the colonies there. This is not only the most splendid portion of the American story, but so much detached, that it forms a perfect whole by itself, remarkable for the unity of the subject. As the principles and maxims of the Spaniards in planting colonies, which have been adopted in some measure by every nation in Europe, are unfolded in this part of my work; it will serve as a proper introduction to the history of their establishment in America.[1]

---

1. William Robertson, *The History of America*, vol. 1 (London: W. Strahan & T. Cadell, 1777), vi.

When reading the quote, you might have been surprised that by "America," Robinson did not mean the United States of America, which didn't exist yet. Instead, "America" for Robertson constituted a geographical and cultural unity that encompassed both major landmasses, including lands colonized by the Spanish and "every nation in Europe." Clearly, then, like Europe, America as a "big idea" has not had consistent meaning over time. For Robinson, the idea of America entailed a metageography that assumed that the subjugation of the lands in the Western Hemisphere to European colonialism was a positive outcome of history. Thus, he started his *History of America* not with the origins of native peoples (a subject addressed only by chapter 4), but with explorations and conquests starting with the ancient Egyptians, Greeks, and Romans. For Robertson, "America" as an idea only existed as the subject of European efforts to expand empire.

A second feature of Robertson's book was that he imagined the indigenous peoples of the Americas as homogenous. There was no need to recognize the distinct cultures and societies of America's native peoples, Robertson explained, since "all the different tribes have such a near resemblance, that they may be painted with the same features."[2] Robertson explained that there were people who he called "Californians" and "Eskimaux" (even though neither name was used by any native peoples to describe themselves).[3] Yet he also claimed (incorrectly) that all Americans looked the same and shared a feeble intellect, a tendency toward sentimentality, and a weak physical constitution.[4] In short, Robertson's characterization of Americans was both condescending and naïve.

When the era of colonial conquest that Robinson's book celebrated began—in 1492—the idea of "America" did not exist. The captain of the expedition that year that brought the first Christians to this region of the world—a seaman named Cristoforo Colombo (you probably know him by another name, but I'll come back to that point)—always thought he sailed to Asia. Colombo called these lands the "Indies," a term that originated in the Greek name for territories east of the Indus River—including India, Southeast Asia, and China. The word "America" first appeared in Freiburg-im-Breisgau, a city in the Holy Roman Empire, sitting between the Rhine River and the Black Forest, in present-day southwestern Germany. In 1507, a mapmaker there, Martin Waldseemüller (perhaps in cooperation with a partner, Matthias Ringmann), used it in his newly published description of the earth. The author, in mapping and describing lands

---

2. Robertson, *The History of America*, 283.

3. The French borrowed the term "Eskimaux" for the Inuit from the Ojibwa people. For a discussion of this, William C Sturtevant, *Handbook of North American Indians*, vol. 5, Arctic (Washington, DC: Smithsonian Institution, 1984), 5–7.

4. Robertson, *The History of America*, 308–40.

in the southern part of the Western Hemisphere, explained that he chose to call the territory America, or "the land of Americus," in honor of Amerigo Vespucci (1454–1512), the first Christian to establish that these lands were not Asia, but a landmass previously unknown to residents of Christendom.[5] Originally, Waldseemüller intended the term to apply only to the southern landmass (mostly present-day Brazil) where Vespucci visited. But within a few decades most authors in the lands of Christendom used the term "America" to refer to both landmasses. In coming years, people living in Christendom called these lands "America," the "Americas," "the West Indies" (as distinguished from what they started calling the "East Indies," which Colombo had intended to find), or simply as the "New World." In all cases, the terminology was self-referential—the lands only had meaning relative to their relationship to Christian worldviews of the late fifteenth and early sixteenth centuries.

Meanwhile, none of the vastly diverse peoples from the Inuit in the far north to the Mapuche people living in the far south used "the Indies," "America," or the "New World" to describe where they lived. This does not mean that all these groups were isolated from one another. For example, the Hopewell exchange system constituted a complex network of peoples lasting from about 200 BCE to about 500 CE and stretching from present-day New York and Ontario to as far south as the Gulf of Mexico and as far west as present-day Kansas. But there was no single worldview, language, or economic network tying all these peoples together.[6] Even using a term like "Native Americans" to refer to them in the years before 1492 is problematic, because it implies some unity, shared experience, or common characteristics. Some peoples living on these large landmasses of the earth later built shared identities based on common experiences, but those only developed (as we'll see later in this chapter) as a result of their interactions with the newly arriving conquerors and colonists coming from across the eastern ocean.

My point in discussing terminology, and this chapter's unusual use of names—calling people usually described as Europeans "Christians" or a man you probably know as Christopher Columbus as Cristoforo Colombo—is that the conventional words that we have in English to tell the story of these early interactions only developed their meanings after the fact as a result of the outcomes of those interactions.[7] When Colombo set sail from the Spanish port of Palos de la

---

5. Martin Waldseemüller, *Cosmographia Introductio* (Strasbourg, 1509), C2r. Accessed at Münchner DigitalisierungsZentrum, www.digitale-sammlungen.de.

6. Charles C. Mann, *1491: New Revelations of the Americas before Columbus*, (New York: Vintage Books, 2011).

7. By the time the he set sail, he called himself Christóbal Colón. When living in Portugal, he had used the name Cristovao Colombo. Charles C. Mann, *1493: Uncovering the New World Columbus Created* (New York: Knopf, 2011), 14.

Frontera there still were no Europeans, at least not in the sense that we use that term now. When Colombo arrived on an island that today lies in the Bahamas, there were no Americans either. Both terms were retrospective inventions. It was only much later that anyone adopted the terms "American Indian" or "Native American" to describe themselves.

At the same time, the experience of learning about (and conquering) the "Americas" contributed to the creation of the idea of "Europe." Thus, in chapter 1, I emphasized the importance of the Reformation and the religious wars that followed it in transforming Christendom into a new idea of Europe over the course of about a century and a half. The two main arguments in this chapter build on those earlier ideas. First, I argue that the creation of the idea of Europe was not just a result of events internal to Europe, but was also tied to global processes, including the conquest and colonization of the Americas. That is, the invention of "America" and the invention of "Europe" were interrelated developments. "Europe" as an idea only ever arose as the outcome of choices made by people all over the world that resulted in Europeans emerging as dominant global actors economically, politically, and culturally.

Second, I argue that the creation of America during the colonial era (depicted in Map 2.1) helps us understand some of the most influential forced migrations in world history, which themselves sparked new waves of refugees fleeing hardship, oppression, and subjugation. Some of these refugees may be those you expect: Protestants escaping religious intolerance back in Europe. But far more significant numbers of refugees were peoples fleeing the brutal enslavement, environmental collapse, social breakdown, and military assaults of European colonialism. Far more refugees, that is, were Africans (or creoles of African descent) and indigenous peoples who fled very real threats—slavery, disease, invasion, and hunger—than Protestants fleeing Europe. As colonization transformed the lives of indigenous populations and involuntary African migrants alike, refugees among these groups helped form new hybridized societies—some that seriously challenged the colonial order and others that strengthened it.

The Invention of America

The invention of America—usually associated with the moment that Colombo stumbled upon an Arawak settlement in the Bahamas—was largely accidental.[8] Leaders of Christian states had been funding long-distance trade missions for centuries before 1492, usually guided by an interest in accessing trade markets

---

8. Edmundo O'Gorman, *The Invention of America* (Bloomington: Indiana University Press, 1961). J. H. Elliott, *The Old World and the New, 1492–1650* (Cambridge: Cambridge University Press, 1970).

MAP 2.1 The Americas in the Seventeenth Century

in China and India. However, just as the boundaries of Christendom were being solidified, the Portuguese stepped up their efforts to expand their trade networks. Why? In part, the Portuguese king was inspired by the kind of crusading spirit that we learned about in chapter 1. The Renaissance Pope Nicholas V even issued a papal bull granting King Afonso (1432–1481) the right to enslave Muslims and so-called pagans (a pejorative term for nonmonotheists) whom his men encountered in North Africa.[9] In addition, Afonso's uncle Henrique, duke of Viseu (1394–1460), was interested in this exploration because he was fascinated with

9. Norman Housley, *Religious Warfare in Europe 1400–1536* (Oxford: Oxford University Press, 2002), 187.

rumors that a descendant of one of the three kings who supposedly visited Jesus after his birth had founded a kingdom in East Africa.[10] But King Afonso was primarily interested in accessing the lucrative trade in luxury goods of the Silk Roads and the Indian Ocean world, which Europeans had accessed for centuries only through intermediary merchants, including Gujaratis from the Indian subcontinent and Arabs living in the Ottoman Empire and Mamluk Egypt.[11] The Portuguese hoped that they might find their way around Africa, to tap into markets in India and China directly.

In pursuit of this dream, Duke Henrique expanded Portuguese exploration southward along the African coast. During these early efforts he claimed various islands off the coast of Africa, including Madeira, the Azores, and the Cape Verde Islands. By the 1440s, Henrique's explorers had established small colonies on these islands. He also began the Portuguese kingdom's first purchase of sub-Saharan African slaves—many of whom they bought from the Wolof Empire, which sold soldiers captured in battles to the Portuguese. The Portuguese forced these enslaved people to produce sugar on plantations in the new colonies.[12] From the mid-fifteenth century, then, we see the signs of an economic system that used slave labor of forced migrants (Africans) to turn raw materials (sugar cane) into commodities (sugar) in colonies (these Atlantic islands) for sale to wealthy elites back in the lands that today we call Europe. This system, which we usually associate with American colonialism, actually preceded it.

By traveling westward across the Atlantic, Colombo was attempting to copy Portuguese sailors, who themselves only made it to Asia because of a mishap. In 1487, a Portuguese ship captained by Bartolomeu Dias (1450–1500) sailed from Lisbon down the west coast of Africa. A storm accidentally forced the ship around the Cape of Good Hope, proving that a water route to Asia around Africa was possible. Within a decade, Portuguese traders started bringing home rich cargos of spices, drugs, jewels, and pearls from India and beyond. Other Christian kingdoms aimed to copy the Portuguese successes. But after Dias's voyage, Cristoforo Colombo's (1451–1506) journey into the Atlantic Ocean in 1492 was still not inevitable, but the result of another accident of history. It just so happens that news of the Portuguese discovery of a new route to Asian markets made its way to the Spanish court at about the same time that the king and queen were on the verge of conquering the Emirate of Granada (discussed in chapter 1). This convergence proved fortuitous for Columbo, who had been arguing for years

10. John K. Thornton, *A Cultural History of the Atlantic World, 1250–1820* (Cambridge: Cambridge University Press, 2012), 16–17.

11. Milo Kearney, *The Indian Ocean in World History* (New York: Routledge, 2004), 57–101.

12. Mann, *1493*, 291–98. Sidney W. Mintz, *Sweetness and Power: The Place of Sugar in Modern History* (New York: Viking, 1985), 30–73.

(mistakenly) that the globe was much smaller than most believed, and thus that a journey across the Atlantic would be fairly easy. After an exhausting war conquering the Iberian peninsula and eager to compete with Portugal, King Ferdinand and Queen Isabella agreed to support his expedition. Colombo departed in August 1492. Thirty-three days later, he made landfall in the Bahamas.

The voyages of Bartolomeu Dias and Cristoforo Colombo marked a new phase of world history characterized by increasing exploration of the earth by agents of Christian states. Of course, at the time, no one realized the magnitude of their actions, and there were many moments when the outcome could have been quite different. Dias's navigation error might have resulted in the sinking of his ship. Ferdinand and Isabella might have taken longer to defeat the Emirate of Granada and never met Colombo. Or they might have concluded that the investment wasn't wise because the sailor's calculations about the size of the earth were faulty. But these events did take place, and they transformed the world in ways that no one could have imagined.

In the century that followed, Christian explorers—Portuguese, Spanish, French, Dutch, English, and others—met different kinds of peoples all over the planet, who became connected to one another (whether they knew it or not) economically, politically, and culturally. Some initial encounters were peaceful and respectful, especially when the travelers felt vulnerable or outnumbered. But time after time, misunderstandings, accidents, threats, and provocations turned to violence. The anthropologist Jarod Diamond has argued that technological disparities—rooted in different geological opportunities that promoted the formation of metallurgy—were a chief reason for the conquest and political domination that followed.[13] Diamond correctly points to the potential for injuring and killing afforded by swords, guns, and cannons, as well as horses and armor, which made slaughters of populations across the Western Hemisphere by visitors from the Eastern Hemisphere more likely. That useful contextualization, however, does not sufficiently account for the decisions that ordinary people made about how they used those weapons. Consider two brief examples. On Colombo's second voyage in 1494, after he saw Arawak villagers dying from an epidemic, he could have ordered his men back to their ships until he figured out what was going on. Instead, he sent them out searching for gold. Later, when Colombo got ill, his soldiers went on a rampage, stealing, killing, raping, and torturing. By the time their captain recovered, more than 50,000 Arawak were dead. Did he withdraw from their island and rethink his approach? No, he reorganized his soldiers to kill and enslave the people in a more orderly manner. My point is not to dwell on the morality of those choices, but to point out that they were decisions that people could have made otherwise. Of course, not all the deaths were the results

---

13. Jared Diamond, *Guns, Germs, and Steel: The Fates of Human Societies* (New York: Norton, 1997), 71–74.

of human choices. Smallpox, measles, and other diseases previously unknown in the Western Hemisphere devastated populations as well. Still, colonial conquests across the Americas were by no means inevitable.

From here on out, I will refer to the Christians from the large western peninsula of Eurasia as "Europeans," to acknowledge the transformation taking place that I described in chapter 1. But I also want to recognize another conclusion that should be clear by now: developing a self-awareness of being European was connected to an awareness of and participation in colonial conquest. At the start, becoming "European" also entailed developing a sense of superiority over non-Europeans, and seeing people Europeans called "Americans" as homogenous and inferior.[14] For these early Europeans, America was less a homeland for thousands of diverse cultures and more a place to extract silver and gold or to cultivate crops like sugar and tobacco to serve the material well-being of competing European peoples. That is, at the start the new ideas of "Europe" and "America" entailed a relationship between them: a self-identity as "Europeans" implied conquest of "Americans."[15] Those concepts emerged retrospectively to explain outcomes that might well have turned out some other way.

European Refugees in the Americas

Just as with the creation of Europe, the creation of America brought with it destabilizing refugee crises and other massive displacements of people. Probably the most famous group of "refugees" associated with early America were the English Puritans who founded Massachusetts Bay Colony in 1630. But we need to be careful about exaggerating the case.[16] It turns out that Puritan views were only shared by a minority of colonists to New England, the vast majority of whom came to enrich themselves, not to flee persecution.[17] Many colonists also happily returned home,

---

14. Christian F. Feest, "The Collecting of American Indian Artifacts in Europe, 1493–1750," in *America in European Consciousness, 1493–1750*, ed. Karen Ordahl Kupperman (Chapel Hill: University of North Carolina Press, 1995), 324–60. Carina Johnson, *Cultural Hierarchy in Sixteenth-Century Europe: The Ottomans and Mexicans* (Cambridge: Cambridge University Press, 2011), 115–16.

15. Other factors helped define "Europe" as well, including its relationship with a place Europeans came to call the "East," which today we call the Middle East and Asia.

16. In the nineteenth-century United States, a heroic memory of Puritans as refugees served a kind of "invented tradition" that helped build a national identity both to help heal the wounds of the Civil War and to imagine the United States as a nation of immigrants. For Thanksgiving in this process of myth-making, see Elizabeth Pleck, "The Making of the Domestic Occasion: The History of Thanksgiving in the United States," *Journal of Social History* 32, no. 4 (1999): 773–89.

17. W. A. Speck and L. Billington, "Calvinism in Colonial North America, 1630–1715," in *International Calvinism, 1541–1715*, ed. Menna Prestwich (Oxford: Clarendon Press, 1985), 257–83.

or moved back and forth between Europe and the colonies. Those Puritans who put religious priorities first were less refugees escaping persecution and more idealists who aimed to build a new Christian utopia, including being willing to persecute those who threatened their vision. Antitolerationism remained dominant in Puritan New England.[18] Their aim was to extend the intolerant logic described in chapter 1. Neither were the Puritans fleeing state-sponsored persecution in any straightforward sense. It's true that English dissenters faced fines if they refused to attend states-sponsored churches, but the executions for heresy that had occurred a century before were a thing of the past. Further, the king of England, Charles I, explicitly granted permission for the creation of Massachusetts Bay.[19] It is true that Puritan preachers drew on biblical themes of exile in their sermons. In 1679 the Boston pastor Increase Mather wrote, "There never was a Generation that did so perfectly shake off the dust of Babylon . . . as the first Generation of Christians, that came into this Land [New England] for the Gospels sake."[20] Seeing the migration to New England as a mirror of the ancient Israelites' exile in Babylon served as a useful rhetorical tool for the fiery preacher, whose goal was to shame listeners whose religious commitment, he felt, had grown weak. But using biblical exile as a metaphor for urging self-sacrifice was a theme common for many Christian writers. We should not confuse such rhetoric with the actual experience of persecution and exile.

A more straightforward case of Reformation-era refugees who fled to the North American colonies were the French Protestant exiles. In 1685, the French king, Louis XIV, revoked the edict of toleration that had been issued to resolve more than a generation of warfare and violence between Catholics and Protestants. Some 150,000 refugees fled, including some who went to South Carolina, New York, and Virginia. The records those refugees left behind emphasized the noble suffering of pious Christians. But their accounts also left out inconvenient facts that betrayed a more ambiguous reality, including sometimes their close relationships with Catholics as well as their own decidedly un-pious behavior. Of course, there was good incentive for these refugees to omit unappealing details. They wrote these memoirs often in order to gain financial and material support from their hosts.[21] Scholars have debated the extent to which those

---

18. Andrew R. Murphy, *Conscience and Community: Revisiting Toleration and Religious Dissent in Early Modern England and America* (University Park: Penn State University Press, 2001).

19. *The Charters and General Laws of the Colony and Province of Massachusetts Bay* (Boston: T. B. Wait, 1814), 2

20. Increase Mather, *A Call from Heaven to the Present and Succeeding Generations* (Boston: John Foster, 1679), 57.

21. Carylyn Lougee Chappel, "Writing the Diaspora: Escape Memoirs and the Construction of Huguenot Memory," in *L'Identité huguenote: Faire mémoire et écrire l'histoire (XVIe–XXIe siècle)*, ed. Philip Benedict, Hugues Daussy, and Pierre-Olivier Léchot (Geneva: Librarie Droz, 2014), 261–77.

French Protestant exiles maintained a vital identity in the Americas, with Jon Butler rather pessimistic and Susanne Lachenicht more positive.[22] However, it's useful to note that only about 2,000 Huguenot exiles ever fled to British North America, and those who did were often pushed to do so in the face of xenophobia and mistrust from fellow Protestants in England. In short, Protestant refugees from Europe played a relatively small role in the history of colonialism in the Americas.

We find a slightly different situation when we consider Muslims and Jews (and people of Muslim and Jewish descent) in the Spanish and Portuguese empires. The possibility that heresies might creep into the colonies provoked deep anxieties among government and church officials, about how to maintain religious purity while engaging in global territorial expansion.[23] A number of moriscos— Muslims who had been forcibly converted to Christianity—came to the Americas as slaves, soldiers, or sailors. Once they crossed the ocean, some escaped from their masters or overseers—we might well call some of these people refugees. Similarly, conversos—people born Jewish who were forcibly converted or whose ancestors had been forcibly converted—who fled to the Americas faced scrutiny when they demonstrated views that challenged Christian norms.[24] The Spanish government established inquisitions in Mexico City and Lima in 1570 and Cartagena de Indias in 1610. When judges determined that conversos were practicing secret Judaism in the colonies, as was the case with Luis de Carvajal "the Younger" in 1596, offenders could be burned.[25] But Jewish and Muslim refugees played a greater role in colonial officials' imagination than they ever played in the reality of American colonialism, in which they were only ever a very minor factor.

African Refugees in the Americas

Much more significant forced migrations resulting from the invention of America were the massive involuntary relocations associated with the African slave trade. During the time that it functioned, over fifteen million people were

---

22. Jon Butler, *The Huguenots in America: A Refugee People in New World Society* (Cambridge, MA: Harvard University Press, 1983). Susanne Lachenicht, *Hugenotten in Europa und Nordamerika: Migration und Integration in der Frühen Neuzeit* (Frankfurt: Campus Verlag, 2010).

23. Karoline P. Cook, *Forbidden Passages: Muslims and Moriscos in Colonial Spanish America* (Philadelphia: University of Pennsylvania Press, 2016).

24. Stuart Schwartz, *All Can Be Saved: Religious Toleration and Salvation in the Iberian Atlantic World* (New Haven, CT: Yale University Press, 2008).

25. Martin A. Cohen, *The Martyr: Luis de Carvajal, A Secret Jew in Sixteenth-Century Mexico* (Albuquerque: University of New Mexico Press, 2001).

forcibly moved from sub-Saharan Africa to the Americas. The African slave trade was one of the most historically significant forced migrations in world history not just for its demographic impacts, but also for its cultural, economic, and political implications for centuries. As we have seen, the African slave trade predated Europeans' arrival in the Americas by decades. Initially, Europeans in the Americas mostly enslaved indigenous people to perform coerced labor. However, a massive decline of this forced labor pool in the Americas (caused by disease and brutal working conditions) brought the enslavement of Africans and the colonization of the Americas together: in 1501 Europeans started purchasing enslaved peoples from markets along the West African coast to work in American fields and mines where indigenous populations were severely declining.

By the 1550s, while most enslaved laborers in the Americas were still indigenous people, Africans—mostly from the areas between present-day Senegal and Niger—had become a significant part of the labor force.[26] (It's important to note that none of these people identified as "African"—a point we'll return to in chapter 5.) In Spanish and Portuguese colonies, enslaved Africans worked in silver and gold mines, but also on plantations growing sugar (and later other cash crops). The English, Dutch, and French later adopted similar systems of slave labor in their American colonies as well. By the seventeenth century tens of thousands of people per year were sold into slavery, often in gruesome working conditions. The violence perpetrated on individuals to maintain slavery on that massive scale sent shock waves through history.

Enslaved Africans were not refugees, though, but forced migrants of another kind entirely. The refugees we learned about in chapter 1 were voluntary migrants, in the sense that they fled their homes facing persecution. Their choices were made out of real fears—death, physical punishment, conversion, or rebellion—but they were *choices*. The Africans sold into slavery did not decide to leave their homes; millions of men and women were sold by African traders to European slavers, forced onto ships for periods of two weeks to five months, and sold off as property in a world that was wholly unfamiliar to them. The experience was profoundly traumatic. They did not know where they were, or how to get back. One group of runaways fleeing slavery in South Carolina just started walking east, hoping to reach their homes back in the Congo River basin. Another group built a canoe hoping to sail back home.[27] Sometimes, all that enslaved people had in common with one another was their shared disorientation and oppression. The point here is not to compare which people faced worse conditions, but to clarify

---

26. Herbert S. Klein, *The Atlantic Slave Trade* (Cambridge: Cambridge University Press, 1999), 17–46.

27. Stephanie E. Smallwood, *Saltwater Slavery: A Middle Passage from Africa to American Diaspora* (Cambridge, MA: Harvard University Press, 2007), 184.

the difference between refugees—people who fled hardship, persecution, or punishment—from those people who were captured and sold into slavery. Both types of migrations were coerced, to be sure, but the nature of their condition is rather distinct. Still, learning a bit about the conditions of slavery will help understand the communities of African refugees that did emerge in the Americas.

Several key commonalities characterized the various systems of mass slavery across the Americas: enslaved Africans were psychologically traumatized by the experience, enslaved people were weakened by poor health conditions, high death rates required slave owners to constantly replace slaves with new African captives, enslaved peoples deeply resented their masters, and slave owners frequently resorted to violence to suppress dissent. As one Maryland slave owner confessed, he had "never known a single instance of a negro being contented in slavery."[28] The myth of the happy and docile slave, which you may have heard about at some point, only emerged in the nineteenth century.

And yet enslaved Africans had a wide variety of experiences living in the Americas.[29] In some cases, slaves worked in small, isolated groups, under the close supervision of their owners. Such was the case on tobacco farms, where enslaved Africans were likely to learn a European language and to have sexual and other personal relations with free Euro-Americans. On the other hand, they were also unlikely to be able to escape as refugees. Other enslaved Africans worked in medium- or large-scale gangs on plantations (the most common was sugar) and in mines (the most common was silver). Gang labor usually used mostly adult male slaves. In these situations, Africans had few relations with Euro-Americans, and built more African-influenced hybrid cultures. Death rates for enslaved Africans were usually worse in situations of gang labor. But they were high everywhere. In Virginia, where tobacco was the central crop, roughly a quarter of enslaved people died within a year. Not far away in Carolina, where slave owners used gangs for work on rice plantations, roughly a third of Africans died within the year.[30] It was also easier for people to run away from labor gangs, because they were under less direct supervision, so they were more able to help one another escape.

In time, many slaves built whole new societies for themselves. They sometimes formed fictive kin groups among fellow enslaved people or people who had survived the harrowing voyage across the ocean with them.[31] While enslaved

---

28. Quoted in Philip D. Morgan, *Slave Counterpoint: Black Culture in the Eighteenth-Century Chesapeake and Lowcountry* (Chapel Hill: University of North Carolina Press, 1998), 278.

29. Michael L. Conniff and Thomas J. Davis, *Africans in the Americas: A History of the Black Diaspora* (New York: St. Martin's Press, 1994), 48–58. Morgan, *Slave Counterpoint*.

30. Smallwood, *Saltwater Slavery*, 193. Morgan, *Slave Counterpoint*, 444–45.

31. Morgan, *Slave Counterpoint*, 448.

Africans spoke diverse languages, many were able to communicate with one another.[32] After all, many sub-Saharan African languages shared enough grammar, sounds, or meanings that people could learn to understand one another. Plus multilingualism was fairly common in most regions of sub-Saharan Africa. Given the continent's linguistic diversity, many people used vehicular languages (also called *lingua francas*), languages whose central purpose is to allow those who speak different languages to communicate with one another for trade, diplomacy, or other forms of cross-cultural exchange. Often enslaved Africans developed their own creole languages that served this purpose.

One of the most common forms of association in the new hybrid societies of Africans in the Americas developed between people of the same region. That sometimes meant that people from rival neighboring kingdoms back in Africa— who might have been enemies back home—became allies in the Americas, often because their languages were similar. Sometimes religion also provided the basis for the creation of new hybrid cultures. Before 1580, a large proportion of slaves in Portuguese colonies came from the region between the Senegal River and Cape Mount (in present-day Liberia). Many of these were Muslims from the Jolof Confederation, made up of the Mandingo, Fula, Jolof, and Tukulor peoples.[33] Their shared belief in Islam could tie them together. Similarly, many belief systems from the Mbundu people of present-day Angola became common in much of seventeenth-century Brazil. Central African forms of divination and healing also emerged within religious systems that operated alongside forms of Christianity that they learned in the Americas. In some places, associations of enslaved peoples who shared cultural and social forms came to be called "nations." In Brazil, the most important nations were Angola, Mina (or Nago), and Nigeria-Benin. As the historian James Sweet has shown, these people recreated or adapted elements of African ritual systems and beliefs in the Americas.[34] Nations provided charity for fellow slaves in need, and served other social and religious functions. They could also become centers of organized resistance or help people flee slavery.

Many thousands of people who fled the persecution and oppression of slavery for freedom can properly be called refugees. Runaways, commonly called "maroons," formed havens of refugees from slavery in the hills, swamps, and forests around large colonial settlements all across the Americas. The first maroon communities were established only shortly after African slavery in the Americas started; the earliest case appears in 1503 on the island of Hispaniola. They were

---

32. Smallwood, *Saltwater Slavery*, 118. Morgan, *Slave Counterpoint*, 561–62.

33. James H. Sweet, *Recreating Africa: Culture, Kinship, and Religion in the African-Portuguese World, 1441–1770* (Chapel Hill: University of North Carolina Press, 2003), 87–101.

34. Sweet, *Recreating Africa*.

most common around places where gang labor was prominent, because cooperation between enslaved peoples to help one another escape was easier there and
working conditions the most brutal. A Spanish colonist in Cuba, Hernando de
Castro, reported in 1543 from the city of Santiago that maroon communities
established in the wilderness served as sites of resistance to slavery. Maroon refugees often burned colonists' ranches, killed slave-owning colonists, and rescued
enslaved people.[35]

Maroon communities arose all through the Americas—in British, Spanish,
Portuguese, French, and Dutch colonies alike. They were variously known as
palenques, quilombos, mocambos, cumbres, ladeiras, and *mambises.* In the British
colonies, maroon communities could be found in Jamaica, Carolina, Virginia,
Georgia, and elsewhere.[36] The most famous maroon community in the present-
day lands of the United States was in Dismal Swamp, on the Virginia-North
Carolina border, later made famous for its portrayal in an 1856 novel by the
American author, Harriet Beecher Stowe. In *Dred: A Tale of the Great Dismal
Swamp,* the character for whom the book is named is a maroon who helps run-
away slaves.[37] Dismal Swamp's challenging geography allowed it to host as many
as 2,000 maroons at its height. Mostly, though, maroon communities were between 100 and 300 residents, usually located in a well-defensible location that
had reliable access to water and arable land. Maroon communities had more men
than women, probably because men were more commonly sold into slavery in the
first place, as a result of both supply and demand forces.[38] But women played a
prominent role in some maroon societies, including sometimes serving as leaders.

Historians do not agree about how frequently maroon communities formed
around coherent ethnic identities. John Thornton argues that this was common,
though Alvin O. Thompson has suggested that most maroon communities were
ethnically mixed. They might have developed a shared vehicular language and
religious traditions, Thompson admits, while maintaining substantial ethnic
diversity.[39] Sometimes maroons joined communities of indigenous Americans,

---

35. José Franco, "Maroons and Slave Rebllions in the Spanish Territories," in *Maroon Societies:
Rebel Slave Communities in the Americas,* ed. Richard Price (Baltimore: Johns Hopkins
University Press, 1996), 50.

36. Sylviane A. Diouf, *Slavery's Exiles: The Story of American Maroons* (New York: New York
University Press, 2014).

37. Harriet Beecher Stowe, *Dred: A Tale of the Great Dismal Swamp* (Boston: Phillips,
Sampson and Co., 1856).

38. Alvin O. Thompson, *Flight to Freedom: African Runaways and Maroons in the Americas*
(Kingston: University of the West Indies Press, 2006), 67–78.

39. John Thornton, *Africa and Africans in the Making of the Atlantic World, 1400–1800,*
2nd ed. (Cambridge: Cambridge University Press, 1998), 201–02. Thompson, *Flight to
Freedom,* 78–88.

whose populations were in retreat and also faced enslavement by European colonists. The Miskito people of present-day Honduras and Nicaragua welcomed maroon refugees fleeing English Puritans' Providence Island Colony in the Caribbean in the mid-seventeenth century. Over time the two communities fused into a single hybrid society.[40] Of course, a central problem facing researchers who study maroons is that most primary sources that survive for historians were produced by European enslavers, who had poor understandings about maroon identities, so we may never have all the answers in this debate.

In some cases, maroon colonies even gained recognition from European states. The Esmeraldas colony of maroons was established after a slave ship was lost off the coast of Ecuador. By the end of the sixteenth century, its leader, known as Francisco de Arobe, depicted in Figure 2.1, signed a peace treaty with Spain, which granted the maroons practical autonomy in exchange for formally recognizing Spanish authority.[41] Maroons could also form strategic alliances with European colonists. Following a 1739 agreement in Jamaica, the Windward

FIGURE 2.1 Francisco de Arobe (middle) was the leader of a hybrid maroon community called Esmeraldas, located on the north coast of Ecuador. This painting was commissioned two years after he signed a treaty with Spain.

---

40. Mary W. Helms, *Asang: Adaptations to Culture Contact in a Miskito Community* (Gainsville: University of Florida Press, 1971).

41. On the balance between collaboration and conflict between Esmeraldas and Spain, see Charles Beatty-Medina, "Caught between Rivals: The Spanish-African Maroon Competition for Captive Indian Labor in the Region of Esmeraldas during the Late Sixteenth and Early Seventeenth Centuries," *Americas: A Quarterly Review of Inter-American Cultural History* 63, no. 1 (2006): 113–36.

Maroons helped British colonists hunt down people fleeing slavery in exchange for land and limited rights as British subjects.[42]

In a few cases, maroon communities became large autonomous kingdoms of their own. One remarkable example is Palmares, in northeastern Brazil.[43] The community was established by maroon refugees in about 1605–1606. Palmares was apparently Bantu-speaking; that is, while all community members did not come from the same region or culture, most came from regions with enough shared linguistic heritage that they could communicate in a tongue other than Portuguese. Records suggest that more than ten thousand refugees lived there at a given time.[44] Palmares had an elected monarchy and an established social hierarchy modeled on Bantu-style political organizations in sub-Saharan Africa. Its capital city at Macaco had a church, council house, many buildings, and several iron foundries.[45] It became a center for ongoing acts of rebellion and resistance to Portuguese rule through the seventeenth century and its fortifications were strong enough to repel more than twenty Portuguese invasions between 1643 and 1677. The 715-square-mile territory was defended by two palisade fences with gates and a ditch filled with wooden spikes.[46] As in other maroon communities, sentries stood guard, passwords were required for entry, and scouts and spies warned the community of impending dangers.

Maroon communities were sometimes places to organize resistance to slavery throughout the Americas. Refugees plotted large-scale revolts. This was the case in Saint-Domingue (later renamed Haiti) in the 1520s, Venezuela and Panama in the 1550s, and Suriname and Jamaica in the 1680s and 1690s. The deadliest slave revolt in North America—the Stono Rebellion of 1739—was led by slaves from South Carolina fleeing to join maroon refugees living in the town of Mose, in Spanish-ruled Florida.[47] The Haitian Revolution, which broke out in 1791 and ultimately toppled French rule and led to the creation of the first state ruled by formerly enslaved people, counted maroons among its fighters. The first leader of the revolution—an African man named Dutty Boukman—was a maroon from Jamaica.[48] While they

---

42. Kathleen Wilson, "The Performance of Freedom: Maroons and the Colonial Order in Eighteenth-Century Jamaica and the Atlantic Sound," *William and Mary Quarterly*, 3rd Series, 66, no. 1 (2009): 58.

43. R. K. Kent, "Palmares: An African State in Brazil," in *Maroon Societies*, ed. Price, 170–90.

44. Stuart B. Schwartz, *Slaves, Peasants, and Rebels: Reconsidering Brazilian Slavery* (Urbana: University of Illinois Press, 1992), 121.

45. Mann, *1493*, 333.

46. Thompson, *Flight to Freedom*, 187, 92–94.

47. Peter Charles Hoffer, *Cry Liberty: The Great Stono River Slave Rebellion of 1739* (Oxford: Oxford Univeristy Press, 2010).

48. Conniff and Davis, *Africans in the Americas*, 86–86. For a useful discussion of whether maroons developed a revolutionary consciousness, see Thompson, *Flight to Freedom*, 315–22.

had poorer military technology than the Euro-Americans, maroon communities were often filled with experienced soldiers who had served in armies in Africa before being sold into slavery. In addition, some Europeans armed maroons to fight against their imperial rivals.

It would be simplistic and false to paint all maroons as heroic champions of abolitionism. While maroon refugees hated the slave owners, they often also resented those whom they felt were unwilling to abandon a life of servitude. While we might imagine maroons and enslaved people as always having a natural allegiance, at times their resentment for one another surpassed their resentment of slave owners. Surprisingly, some maroons even owned slaves themselves. Meanwhile, some enslaved people proved willing to provide intelligence to slave owners against maroons.[49] These tensions remind us that dividing up the world into neat categories of heroes and villains cannot capture the complexity of history.

American Refugees in the Americas

Another significant kind of refugee emerged as a result of the invention of America: Native Americans fleeing the dangers brought by colonialism. Native peoples of the Americas faced enslavement and death due to disease, more often than expulsion.[50] But as Europeans expanded their colonial conquests in the Americas, many faced forms of forced dislocations. If you grew up in the United States, you may well have learned about the famous Trail of Tears, following the Indian Removal Act of 1830. The US government forcibly removed Cherokee, Seminole, Chickasaw, and other native peoples from their homelands to a land called "Indian Territory" (present-day Oklahoma). Among the various kinds of displacements, however, were refugee crises as well.

As war and disease destabilized communities across the Americas, refugees fleeing danger sometimes refashioned societies altogether. Consider the case of Cuzco, in present-day Peru, where the *mita* system imposed brutal coerced labor on Andean peoples working in the silver mines of Potosí and Huancavelica.[51] Massive waves of refugees began fleeing the harsh system for towns where they were not part of the shared ancestry networks that were used to recruit workers. These refugees, called *forasteros*, made up 50 percent of the population of the bishopric of Cuzco by 1690. Unlike other refugees we have discussed, forasteros

49. Thompson, *Flight to Freedom*, 265–72.

50. Alan Gallay, *The Indian Slave Trade: The Rise of the English Empire in the American South, 1670–1717* (New Haven, CT: Yale University Press, 2002).

51. Mann, *1493*, 142–48.

did not flee Spanish lands entirely. In practice, it turns out, Spanish authorities proved relatively willing to tolerate them to serve roles that needed filling elsewhere in their empire as disease and harsh living conditions were killing off native populations. Forasteros worked as transport and agricultural workers, as artisans and service employees, earning a wage to keep the colonial economy and government running.[52] In the process, they undermined the ancestral ties that had once bound communities together. Though Spanish authorities had always seen forastero refugees as a major destabilizing force that undermined their political power, by the eighteenth century they had in fact helped transform Cuzco into an administrative district of the Spanish empire.

When other indigenous refugees fled diseases, enslavement, and social collapse, they could refashion themselves into powerful threats to colonialism. Consider an example from eastern North America in the mid-seventeenth century, as explained by the historian Stephen Warren.[53] In the Ohio River Valley and the nearby hills, a society that archaeologists call the Fort Ancient Tradition, had maintained a peaceful existence since about 1000 CE, in some of the same lands once dominated by the Hopewell exchange system mentioned earlier in this chapter. The Fort Ancient people spoke a variety of Siouan and Algonquian languages and lived in egalitarian multiethnic settlements of about 250 to 1,000 people, in the summer farming corn in the hills of present-day Kentucky, Ohio, and West Virginia and in the winter hunting and fishing along the Ohio River. In the mid-seventeenth century, though, large-scale waves of refugees from the Fort Ancient society fanned out across eastern North America as their society collapsed. Though the archaeological evidence is not definitive, most scholars now conclude that the Shawnee, a group of itinerant Algonquian-speaking native peoples first recorded by Europeans in 1673, emerged from the Fort Ancient refugee crisis as a major political force in the region.

Historians used to believe that the chief culprit of this flood of refugees were attacks starting in 1667 by the Haudenosaunee—a league of the Iroquoian-speaking Senecas, Oneidas, Cayugas, Onondagas, and Mohawks.[54] There is some truth to this claim. European colonialism on the coast resulted in massive population losses among the Iroquois, as a result of smallpox and measles as well as declining beaver populations. In response, the Haudenosaunee, who had gained early access to valuable Dutch gun markets, began to attack neighboring peoples

---

52. Ann M. Wightman, *Indigenous Migration and Social Change: The Forasteros of Cuzco, 1570–1720* (Durham, NC: Duke University Press, 1990), 111–20.

53. Stephen Warren, *The Worlds the Shawnees Made: Migration and Violence in Early America* (Chapel Hill: University of North Carolina Press, 2014).

54. For an older view, see Richard White, *The Middle Ground: Indians, Empires, and Republics in the Great Lakes Region, 1650–1815* (Cambridge: Cambridge University Press, 1991), 1–49.

to their west to hunt beavers, but more importantly to take captives to replenish their plummeting populations.[55] As it turns out, Iroquois worldviews included a cultural mandate to replace dead relatives with captives from other groups of people, who would assume the deceased's identity.[56] That fact explains why losses due to disease and hunger sparked attacks by Haudenosaunee against their neighbors. In many cases, captives peacefully integrated into these Iroquois-speaking communities. In other cases, the attackers hunted down refugees across vast distances. This violence often sparked warfare, which resulted in Haudenosaunee deaths, which only provoked more raids. In the 1650s, Wyandots, Neutrals, Odawas, Eries, and other peoples were dislocated by Haudenosaunee attacks. Sometimes large groups of refugees fled for safety among neighbors of a different ethnicity. A group of roughly six hundred Wyandots in 1649, for instance, fled to live with the Neutrals. The following year the Haudenosaunee attacked the Neutrals, who were forced to flee with their Wyandot guests. By 1669, the Haudenosaunee also began attacking the Fort Ancient villages along the Ohio River Valley.

Recent archaeological and historical evidence has determined, however, that these attacks were not the main cause of the Fort Ancient refugee crisis. It turns out that by the time that the Haudenosaunee arrived, most Fort Ancient peoples had already abandoned their villages. They had faced major losses due to smallpox and measles outbreaks and slaving expeditions by native peoples (led by Occaneechees and a group known as the Tomahitas), who sold captives to the British. In the face of these disturbances, many Fort Ancient peoples fled their homelands. By the time the Haudenosaunee arrived, the Ohio River Valley was mostly empty of people. The Haudenosaunee took some Fort Ancient peoples captive while others fled as refugees. By the 1680s, the last of the Fort Ancient villages had been abandoned. For decades, the region simply stood empty of humans.

In the wake of these dislocations, the Shawnee emerged as a series of itinerant communities that sprawled across eastern North America. Scholars are uncertain and divided about the extent to which Shawnees existed as a coherent ethnic group before this refugee crisis or emerged only as a result of this crisis out of other groups. Stephen Warren argues that probably both are true. They emerged out of preexisting ethnic groups that formed part of the Fort Ancient Tradition, he concludes, but also easily integrated with other peoples without fundamentally altering their social norms. The example of the Shawnee is one of

---

55. On the way that native peoples used access to gun markets to serve their interests, see David J. Silverman, *Thundersticks: Firearms and the Violent Transformation of Native America* (Cambridge, MA: Belknap Press, 2016).

56. For what follows, see Jon Parmenter, *The Edge of the Woods: Iroquoia, 1534–1701* (East Lansing: Michigan State University Press, 2010).

many challenges to the "myth of the vanishing Indian" that still exists today.[57] In this case, the Fort Ancient Tradition fell apart, but key elements of that culture—values, belief systems, and social structures—survived and adapted, even in the face of the dramatic shocks wrought by European colonialism.

While we might imagine that Shawnees and other Fort Ancient refugees would flee as fast as they could *away* from the forces of European colonialism (epidemics, gun violence, enslavement, and land seizures), the opposite was true. They mostly fled *toward* the colonists. Why might that be? Put yourself in their position for a moment. They concluded—quite rationally—that the only way to survive in this new world was to get access to firearms. They also knew that the only way to purchase guns was to trade for something Europeans did not have: expert knowledge of the geography, languages, and cultures of the region. Thus, Shawnee refugees, like the one depicted in Figure 2.2, established new settlements

FIGURE 2.2 An eighteenth-century European image of a Shawnee man. Source: *Carte générale du cours de la rivière de l'Ohio*, by G. Bois St-Lys and J. J. Boudier (1796). *Source*: Bibliothèque nationale de France

57. Brewton Berry, "The Myth of the Vanishing Indian," *Phylon* 21, no. 1 (1960): 51–57. Matthew Restall, *Seven Myths of the Spanish Conquest* (Oxford: Oxford University Press, 2003), 100–30.

along common travel routes or at the borderlands of European colonies. They became guides, traders, and slavers for Europeans. One group, for instance, emerged as slave traders along the Savannah River (near the present-day site of Augusta, Georgia). Another group of Shawnees settled along the Illinois River, at a settlement known as the Grand Village of the Kaskaskias (about eighty miles southwest of the future city of Chicago). Another Shawnee settlement emerged, populated in part by some who had been in the previous two, around Chesapeake Bay. Wherever Shawnees reinvented themselves, they again lived in multiethnic, multilingual, and largely egalitarian communities, alongside other native peoples.

In the 1720s, Shawnees began moving back to their former homelands in the Ohio River Valley. As other native peoples joined them, they again lived in collections of small multiethnic and un-hierarchical villages.[58] In these new forms of migrant communities, many Shawnees, embittered by decades of colonialism, began to express an "Indian" identity based in a shared history that they defined against the French and English colonists. This harmony was broken during King George's War (a North American extension of Europe's War of the Austrian Succession, 1744–1748), but by the 1750s, the multiethnic communities regained a large degree of autonomy in the Ohio River Valley again. These new communities of forced and voluntary migrants proved a formidable force in North American political developments. In 1763, after the British defeated France in the Seven Years' War (also called the French and Indian War, 1756–1763) and took over its Canadian colony, the dominant European power in the region changed. Shawnees and their allies played an important part in the pan-Indian resistance efforts against the British, including in a conflict that historians usually call "Pontiac's War."[59] The Shawnees became famed for supporting pan-Indian resistance to British colonialism.

In the early nineteenth century, the Shawnees experienced another forced migration. After groups of Euro-American rebels in North America successfully revolted against Great Britain in 1783 and formed the United States of America, the new government's leaders quickly began plans to forcibly remove native peoples to their west.[60] By 1830, the new government had grown into a strong enough position to implement the forced removal of native peoples called the Trail of Tears. Members of the Shawnee diaspora were among those forced into

---

58. After a land fraud in the Pennsylvania colony forced the Delaware people off their land in 1737, they joined the Shawnees in the Ohio River Valley. Some Iroquois speakers who had not allied with the Haudenosaunee joined them. Wyandots fleeing French colonists to the north did as well. Gregory Evans Dowd, *War Under Heaven: Pontiac, the Indian Nations, & the British Empire* (Baltimore: Johns Hopkins University Press, 2002), 38–41.

59. Many historians now admit that this name overestimates the centrality of the Ottawa ruler Pontiac, and undervalues others leaders. Dowd, *War under Heaven*.

60. Thomas Jefferson was an early advocate of forced removals. Anthony F. C. Wallace, *Jefferson and the Indians: The Tragic Fate of the First Americans* (Cambridge, MA: Belknap Press, 1999).

Indian Territory. Unlike the Shawnees' earlier relocations, however, this forced migration was not voluntary but the coercive act of an expanding state—thus more like the African slave trade than the refugee crises covered in this book.

Conclusion

By the time that William Robinson wrote *The History of America*, Europeans had dominated the Western Hemisphere politically, economically, and culturally for centuries. They enslaved and displaced indigenous peoples, affecting social collapse on a massive scale. They imported Africans as slaves to extract labor in the service of European profits. They captured lands, which they primarily treated as resources to be exploited, either for natural resource extraction, the cultivation of cash crops for export, or to sustain colonialism. In that sense, we see remarkable continuity from the days of Martin Waldseemüller: for nearly three centuries, the idea of America only existed relative to European attempts to control this region of the world.

But Robertson's *History of America* also allows us a chance to reflect on changes that had transformed world history in the past three hundred years. First, Robertson used the term "native American" to refer to the indigenous peoples of North and South America. What's interesting is not just that the term imagines a homogenous category of people: Europeans had been imagining "Americans" as pretty undifferentiated for centuries. What is different here is the adjective "native" to distinguish indigenous American peoples from people of European descent. Indeed, by the late eighteenth century, many European creole settlers (people who were born in the colonies but whose ancestors had come from Europe) were calling themselves "American" to distinguish themselves from Europeans. To coopt the term "American," though, they had to stop using it to refer to indigenous people. The term "Native American" emerged in this era to make this distinction. The new understanding of what it meant to be American, that is, constituted a political and racial identity that distinguished the creole settlers of European dissent from Europeans, Africans, and Native Americans— none of whom they now regarded as American.

A second change that we can see in Robertson's book relates to its date of publication: 1777. He wrote it a year after a group of thirteen British colonies declared independence from Great Britain. Recently, on December 26, 1776 and January 3, 1777 the rebels had managed a couple of victories in New Jersey under the leadership of General George Washington.[61] Soon after, Robertson stopped writing his book, which was only half done. In his introduction, he explained

---

61. David G. McCullough, *1776* (New York: Simon & Schuster, 2006).

that the uncertain state of the British North American colonies caused him to abandon his history of America. His decision was telling. Remember that for Robinson, America was an idea of metageography about both of these land-masses that assumed these lands' political, cultural, and economic subservience to Europeans. But by 1777, it was not clear whether America would continue to be a place defined by colonial subjugation. The future of the relationship between Europe and America—one defined relative to its subjugation to the other—looked uncertain. In later years, the idea of America would evolve into a new metageography altogether.

Understanding how and why the ideas of Europe and America were created, the first two chapters of this book argue, helps us make sense of massive disloca-tions and forced migrations that took place from the 1500s into the 1700s in those lands, including a series of refugee crises. Within the lands that were slowly becoming Europe, dislocations of Muslims, Christians, and Jews fractured fami-lies and communities, forged new identities, and ultimately reinforced the idea of an association of states that needed to establish workable relations with people of different faiths. Within the lands that were slowly becoming the Americas, old societies collapsed and new ones formed, indigenous peoples were displaced, millions of Africans were taken from their homes and sold into slavery an ocean away, and millions of Europeans—including a small number of religious refugees fleeing Europe—were emerging as colonial conquerors. In all of these cases, refu-gee movements also led to the creation of new societies. Refugee crises sometimes destroyed old ways and inspired deep resentments, that is, but refugees also fash-ioned for themselves new identities, new alliances, and new cultural forms. As we have seen, there was nothing natural or inevitable about the ideas of Europe and America. As with all big ideas, they were only the product of a history that might have unfolded differently. But they are the ideas that we have inherited from the past and we cannot fully comprehend these early refugee crises without under-standing how they came to be. As we will see in chapter 3, the developments in these first two chapters set the stage for the emergence of another set of big ideas, which became critical to the worst refugee crises of the modern era.

FURTHER READING

Beatty-Medina, Charles. "Caught between Rivals: The Spanish-African Maroon Competition for Captive Indian Labor in the Region of Esmeraldas during the Late Sixteenth and Early Seventeenth Centuries." *Americas: A Quarterly Review of Inter-American Cultural History* 63, no. 1 (2006): 113–36.

Diouf, Sylviane A. *Slavery's Exiles: The Story of the American Maroons.* New York: New York University Press, 2014.

Mann, Charles C. *1493: Uncovering the New World Columbus Created*. New York: Knopf, 2011.

Price, Richard, ed. *Maroon Societies: Rebel Slave Communities in the Americas*. Baltimore: Johns Hopkins University Press, 1996.

Thompson, Alvin O. *Flight to Freedom: African Runaways and Maroons in the Americas*. Kingston: University of the West Indies Press, 2006.

Warren, Stephen. *The Worlds the Shawnees Made: Migration and Violence in Early America*. Chapel Hill: University of North Carolina Press, 2014.

Wightman, Ann M. *Indigenous Migration and Social Change: The Forasteros of Cuzco, 1570–1720*. Durham, NC: Duke University Press, 1990.

3 NATION-STATES AND THE REFUGEE CRISES OF THE GREAT WAR

God gave all men all earth to love
But since our hearts are small,
Ordained for each one spot should prove
Beloved over all; . . .
So one shall Baltic pines content,
As one some Surrey glade,
Or one the palm-grove's droned lament
Before Levuka's Trade.[1]
Each to his choice, and I rejoice
The lot has fallen to me
In a fair ground—in a fair ground—
Yea, Sussex by the sea!

Rudyard Kipling, "Sussex" (1902)[2]

In the poem, the British writer Rudyard Kipling playfully joked with his readers. He began by recognizing that sympathy for one's homeland is not inborn to humans, but a kind of contrivance that we use to prioritize our affinities for those we feel are most like us. Yet he ends by admitting a sincere patriotism. I use this quote to reflect on the most critical change in world history between the end of the previous chapters—roughly the 1770s—and the dawn of the twentieth century. During this period, the nation-state became one of the two dominant forms of political institutions in the world (the other was a colony of a nation-state, which we will turn to in chapter 4). While the leading alternatives—multiethnic empires and local, decentralized governments—still existed in 1902 when Kipling wrote,

---

1. Levuka was the largest settlement and former capital of what was in 1902 the British colony of Fiji, in the Pacific Ocean.

2. The Kipling Society, http://www.kiplingsociety.co.uk/poems_sussex.htm.

within two decades most of the planet had organized either as a nation-state or its colony.[3] This chapter explores how the emergence of the nation-state—our next "big idea"—provoked the largest refugee crises the world had ever seen. It begins by discussing the emergence and changing character of nation-states in Western Europe and the Americas during the so-called long nineteenth century (1780s–1910s). It then looks at examples of refugee crises from the First World War, which allow us to see how these developments promoted destabilizing ideas and outcomes when large multinational empires got suddenly divided up into nation-states.

The Invention of Nation-States

Before getting into the details, let's define our terms, starting with the simplest: the state. The most widely used definition comes from a German sociologist named Max Weber. In January 1919, only a couple months after World War I ended, he defined a state as "the form of human community that (successfully) lays claim to the monopoly of the legitimate physical violence within a given territory."[4] That is, the state is an institution—an empire, democracy, monarchy, or otherwise—that defines what its members can and can't do, and claims a successful enough of a monopoly on power that it can maintain a degree of social, political, economic, and cultural order among its members.

A nation is a bit trickier. In 1983, the philosopher Ernest Gellner offered a useful definition: a nation, he described, requires a shared culture and community, as well as a self-conscious recognition about belonging to that shared culture.[5] Two Inuit hunters living eleven centuries ago—one in Greenland and one in northwestern Canada—might have shared a language and culture, but *they did not know they did*. In contrast, two auto mechanics in the 1950s—one in Atlanta and one in Seattle—shared a common American culture *and knew they did so without ever having met each other*. Another scholar, Benedict Anderson, described nations as "imagined communities."[6] By this he meant a

3. Debate exists on whether some twentieth-century states should be considered nation-states. For the case of China, see Prasanjit Duara, *Rescuing History from the Nation: Questioning Narratives of Modern China* (Chicago: University of Chicago Press, 1995).

4. Max Weber, "Politics as a Vocation," in *The Vocation Lectures,* transl. Rodney Livingstone, ed. David Owen and Tracy Strong (Chicago: Hackett Books, 2004), 33.

5. Ernest Gellner, *Nations and Nationalism* (Ithaca, NY: Cornell University Press, 1983), 1–7.

6. Benedict Anderson, *Imagined Communities: Reflections on the Origin and Spread of Nationalism* (London: Verso, 1991).

nation's members must believe that they belong to a nation for it to exist. Usually, when people identify with one another based on a shared culture, language, and perceived common ancestry, we describe them as having an ethnicity. The idea of nation is distinguished from an ethnicity in that people of a nation believe that their shared identity—sometimes ethnicity but not always—ought to be the basis for their political organization. That is, *the idea of nation implies that one's goal is to create or sustain a nation-state*—a state that is organized around a shared ethnicity, culture, and/or language. For most of human history states existed without nations (the multiethnic Aztec Empire, for instance). Conversely, plenty of nations today exist without a state (for example, the present-day Kurds have been lobbying for a separate state, but live in Turkey, Iraq, Iran, and Syria). A nation-state describes a place where people of a nation have their own state.

When did nation-states first emerge? Usually nationalists—those people who prioritize a commitment to the survival and prosperity of their nation—assert legitimacy for their cause by finding its origins as early as possible. In the process, they have often ignored contrary evidence or misread evidence so that it aligns with their views. Even among scholars, there is no clear agreement. Most historians agree that nation-states are pretty recent. They point out that nineteenth-century nationalists—consciously or unintentionally—invented traditions to make their nation seem older than it was. Two such authors are Eric Hobsbawm and the aforementioned Benedict Anderson.[7] In Scotland, for instance, kilts and tartans became national symbols in the nineteenth century, though nationalists presented them as having ancient roots.[8] During the nineteenth century, nationalists over the world made similar appeals to the distant past, regardless of whether they lived in nation-states, multiethnic empires, or colonies. Other historians, such as Caspar Hirschi, admit that expressions of nationalism are different from earlier forms, but contend that the roots of nationalities trace back centuries.[9] Despite these differences, most historians agree that while some requirements for nations existed before the 1800s, new, more intense forms of nationalism emerged in the nineteenth century in locations all over the world, while nation-states—the dream of nationalists—became especially formidable as political forms in Western Europe and the Americas by the end of that century

---

7. E. J. Hobsbawm, *Nations and Nationalism since 1780: Programme, Myth, Reality* (Cambridge: Cambridge University Press, 1990). Anderson, *Imagined Communities*.

8. Hugh Trevor-Roper, "The Invention of Tradition: The Highland Tradition of Scotland," in *The Invention of Tradition*, ed. Eric Hobsbawm and Terence Ranger (Cambridge: Cambridge University Press, 1983), 15–41.

9. Caspar Hirschi, *The Origins of Nationalism: An Alternative History from Ancient Rome to Early Modern Germany* (Cambridge: Cambridge University Press, 2012).

(at the same time that some of those states engaged in a more intense colonial conquest). How did this happen? Let's take the matter step-by-step. One pre-condition for nation-states is a means to distribute ideas across vast geographical spaces. It might seem self-evident that most members of a country shared their primarily language, but that has not always been so (and in much of the world is not true today). For most of human history, two political forms dominated. Local, decentralized governments (which some people call "tribes" or "clans") had shared language and culture, but there were no institutions connecting people across them, as with the Inuit hunters mentioned earlier. In contrast, in multiethnic empires, an elite ruled over people of multiple languages and cultures. This was the case in the Chinese Empire of East Asia, the Mali Empire of West Africa, and the Russian Empire of Eurasia. It was also true of medieval France and England.

The metal movable-type printing press, invented in Europe in the mid-fifteenth century, proved influential in standardizing languages across vast distances. Initially printed books appeared in Latin—a language shared among educated elites of various cultures in the lands of Christendom. In the sixteenth century, printers began publishing in languages spoken by commoners, including English, French, German, and Spanish. That choice required printers to standardize spelling, which made it easier to reach large audiences, and helped tie literate people together with shared cultural touchstones. By the seventeenth century, weekly and then later daily newspapers—frequent and modestly priced print forms—shared information about current events to an ever-broadening literate public. In the eighteenth century printers began establishing newspapers in cities across Europe, but also in the Americas in places like Boston, Mexico City, and Nova Scotia. Newspapers encouraged readers to see themselves as connected to people and events far away and to feel a part of a large political community. Consider the response to the British Prime Minister Robert Walpole's tax bill in 1733. The act proposed to reduce land taxes (mostly paid by the wealthy) in exchange for higher taxes on tobacco and wine (paid disproportionally by commoners). News of the bill spread like wildfire through newspapers. Unhappy Britons protested, urging representatives in Parliament to vote against the bill, which Walpole retracted. Newspapers became a conduit for individuals not just to learn about politics, but also to participate in it.[10]

This sense of citizen empowerment dramatically expanded during the age of revolutions (1770s–1830s). In many places, citizens called for representative

---

10. G. A. Cranfield, "The 'London Evening Post', 1727–1744: A Study in the Development of the Political Press," *The Historical Journal* 6, no. 1 (1963): 20–37.

governments that could make decisions based on citizens' interests and sense of shared purpose. In Europe, the French Revolution (1789–1799) encouraged a form of citizen-led patriotism that spread across Western Europe. In the American Revolution (1775–1783), many colonists rejected not only monarchy but also European control over their lives. In the Haitian Revolution (1791–1804), new citizens threw off not only colonial rule, but also enslavement. These three revolutions emboldened groups across the Americas, including in the Viceroyalties of New Spain (stretching from present-day California to Costa Rica), Peru (including present-day Peru, Argentina, Uruguay, Paraguay, and Bolivia), and New Granada (present-day Columbia, Ecuador, and Venezuela), which also experienced revolutions that created new nation-states.[11] To sum up: between the 1770s and the 1830s (though mostly only for male, urban elites of European heritage) a new form of political community was emerging. The mass enslavement of populations often persisted, as did the displacement of indigenous peoples, and the disenfranchisement of women. But the idea of active citizens serving as stewards of their own nation-states became a powerful force. Forms of nationalism were also emerging in colonies and multiethnic empires during this period, but only in a few locations outside of Western Europe and the Americas were they accompanied by the creation of the nation-states.[12]

Still, the lure of patriotism was not as obvious as it may seem today. Many, perhaps even most, of those who became members of the new nation-states did not identify as members of their nation. Some did not even realize that they were part of a nation, because they remained illiterate or cut off from educated elites. Others knew that a nation-state existed, but rejected it as irrelevant or an unwelcome annoyance. Still others existed only as "citizens of convenience," happy to embrace whatever nationality served their immediate interests.[13] For most people living within the new nation-states, a sense of national belonging remained distant, secondary, resented, irrelevant, or unknown.

The creation of nation-states, I hope is clear by now, was not the natural outcome of shared cultures that organically emerged out of some primal ooze. Instead, nation-states were the *unintended* consequences of overlapping economic and political developments over centuries. Once they emerged, however, educated urbanites *intentionally and self-consciously* promoted nationalism

---

11. Anthony McFarlane, *War and Independence in Spanish America* (New York: Routledge, 2014).

12. Consider the example of Thailand in Thongchai Winichakul, *Siam Mapped: A History of the Geo-Body of a Nation* (Honolulu: University of Hawaii Press; 1994).

13. Lawrence B. A. Hatter, *Citizens of Convenience: The Imperial Origins of American Nationhood on the U.S.-Canadian Border* (Charlottesville: University of Virginia Press, 2017).

among the masses. Key nineteenth-century inventions, including railroads, radios, telephones, telegraphs, and motion pictures, contributed to the expansion of "imagined communities." Wars and global migration also ensured that forms of nationalism expressed not just positive understandings of communities, but defined themselves against people whose cultures were different. Within nation-states new institutions of education—including schools, armies, and museums—also proved critical to promoting national identities.

Let's start with schools. Around 1800, for most people around the world the government's official language was a foreign tongue. It's not surprising that this was the case in colonies and multiethnic empires, but it was also in the case in most states in Western Europe and Americas as well. In France, for instance, most people did not speak standard French. Some spoke different languages—Dutch/Flemish in the northeast or German in Lorraine—or dialects like Occitan and Walloon that were different enough to make standard French incomprehensible.[14] When the first Parliament of the newly formed nation-state of Italy met in 1861, only two and a half percent of Italians spoke standard Italian. At the time, a cynical politician quipped, "We have made Italy, now we have to make Italians."[15] Across the Americas too—including in the United States—substantial percentages of populations spoke alternative European, indigenous, and African creole languages. Standardizing language among vast populations, promoters of nationalism knew, required a massive investment in public education.

First, governments had to build schools. By 1833, for instance, the French government had built 31,420 public schools. By 1847, that number had doubled.[16] Similar trends emerged elsewhere in Western Europe and the Americas. Having schools was not enough. Governments also had to hire and train the tens of thousands of schoolteachers. But education fails when students reject its value. When students see lessons as irrelevant, they skip classes, neglect their studies, or learn the content only for the test and then promptly forget it. At first, this is just what happened: students saw no use in learning mathematics, history, writing, and patriotism. What changed? Simply put, people started seeing public education as practical. Understanding how to use standard currencies, weights, and measurements allowed them to sell their goods to a national market. To do so, they also had to be able to speak with outsiders. Skills taught in school also allowed them to compete for new government jobs—working in the post office, for instance. By the 1890s, many saw going to school as an investment in their future, rather

---

14. Eugen Weber, *Peasants into Frenchmen: The Modernization of Rural France, 1870–1914* (Stanford, CA: Stanford University Press, 1976), 67–94.

15. Quoted in Hobsbawm, *Nations and Nationalism*, 60.

16. Weber, *Peasants into Frenchmen*, 307.

than an irrelevant waste of time. By the 1910s, most young people across Western Europe and the Americas received a public education that taught them mathematics and reading, but also instilled in them a sense of patriotism.[17]

A similar transformation happened with regard to armies. Early in the nineteenth century, most commoners resented militaries as outside intrusions. The new democratic revolutions across Western Europe and the Americas introduced the idea among urban elites that the rights of citizenship should be tied to a duty to perform military service—an imposition most people resented.[18] In the 1870s and 1880s, governments started massively expanding the sizes of their armies, usually requiring military service from male citizens. Leaders of nation-states also self-consciously promoted military centralization and professionalization.[19] New military colleges were established like the *Collégio militar* in Argentina (f. 1869), the *Escuela Politécnica* in Guatemala (f. 1873), and the US Army War College (f. 1901). To serve these expanding armies, men moved far from their villages, got to know other young men from across the nation, learned the national language, and developed a concern for national affairs. Food and housing were often better in the army than at home. Soldiers also learned skills that helped them succeed in the new economy. They also often became patriotic for the first time. Many soldiers chose not to return to their villages, which probably seemed backward and boring, but moved to cities, took factory jobs, and adopted the lifestyles of cosmopolitan urbanites. Some former soldiers also became schoolteachers, instilling patriotic values in a new generation.

Another way that residents of early nation-states developed national identities was through new celebrations that instilled a sense of a shared history. New museums celebrated nations' imagined shared past. The United States National Museum (f. 1881)[20] belongs to this tradition, but so too does the National Gallery of British Art (f. 1897) and Chile's *Museo Nacional de Bellas Artes* (f. 1880). New holidays also promoted a national culture, in part by pretending it had always been there. Good examples of this are Britain's Royal Navy review (from 1887), the United States' Thanksgiving (from 1863), Bastille Day in France (from 1880), and the day Christopher Columbus is said to have landed

---

17. For examples, see Weber, *Peasants into Frenchmen*, 302–38. Silvina Gvirtz, Jason Beech, and Angela Oria, "Schooling in Argentina," in *Going to School in Latin America*, ed. Silvina Gvirtz and Jason Beech (Westport, CT: Greenwood Press, 2008), 5–34.

18. Alan Forrest, *Conscripts and Deserters: The Army and French Society during the Revolution and Empire* (Oxford: Oxford University Press, 1989).

19. For example, Michael Geyer, "The Past as Future: The German Officers Corps as Profession," in *German Professions, 1800–1950*, ed. Geoffrey Cocks and Konrad H. Jarausch (Oxford: Oxford University Press, 1990), 183–212.

20. Later renamed the Smithsonian Institution's Arts and Industries Building.

in the Americas (celebrated under various names).[21] In school, students learned unblemished stories of national heroes, whether that be Joan of Arc in France, George Washington in the United States, José de San Martín in Argentina, or Martin Luther in Germany. Through these experiences, citizens learned their nation's dominant culture. Millions of parents and grandparents probably felt alienated from their children and grandchildren's unfamiliar lifestyles and world-views. But for those who adopted these new ways of thinking, the changes proba-bly felt exhilarating. Nationalism provided a sense of belonging that transcended factionalisms of earlier eras, promised prosperity, and offered ordinary citizens an unprecedented role in shaping their future.

There was a darker, more exclusionary aspect to these new nation-states, how-ever. Many nineteenth-century nationalists argued that the nation-states did not result from a complex combination of intended and unintended actions over centuries, but were expressions of citizens' biology. Two features of early racial classification schemes stand out. First, each wrongly presented itself as objective, scientific, and universal, though in fact racial categories remained diverse, subjec-tive, and fluctuating. Second, scientists ascribed differences in morality, person-ality, and values to the categories they developed to study humans. In 1785, the German Christoph Meiners divided humans into two categories, Caucasians and Mongolians, adding "that the latter were not only much weaker in body and spirit, but also more inclined toward evil and bereft of virtue."[22] In 1839, though, the American author Samuel George Morton described five races—Caucasians, Mongolians, Malays, Americans, and Ethiopians—each of which he also imagined had distinct physical and moral features.[23] In the 1850s the French race theorist Arthur de Gobineau categorized people by skin color: he described "black" people as bestial and "yellow" people as apathetic and weak, while those he called "white" he imagined were intelligent, strong, and having a natural affinity for freedom.[24]

---

21. Jan Rüger, "Nation, Empire and Navy: Identity Politics in the United Kingdom, 1887–1914," *Past and Present* 185, no. 1 (2004): 159–87. Weber, *Peasants into Frenchmen*, 377–98. Elizabeth Pleck, "The Making of the Domestic Occasion: The History of Thanksgiving in the United States," *Journal of Social History* 32, no. 4 (1999): 773–89. Michel-Rolph Trouillot, *Silencing the Past: Power and the Production of History* (Boston: Beacon Press, 1995), 108–40. Ilan Rachum, "Origins and Historical Significance of Día de la Raza," *European Review of Latin American & Caribbean Studies*, no. 76 (April 2004): 61–81.

22. "*Das Gegenwärtige Menschengeschlecht aus zween Hauptstämmen bestehe, dem Tatarischen oder Kaukasischen, und dem Mongolischen Stamm: daß der letzere nicht nur viel schwächer von Cörper und Geist, sonder auch viel übel garteter und tugendleerer.*" My translation. Christoph Meiners, *Grundriss der Geschichte der Menschheit* (Lemgo: Meyerische Buchhandlung, 1785), unpaginated [B3v].

23. Samuel George Morton, *Crania Americana* (Philadelphia: J. Dobson, 1839), 260–61.

24. Francesco Bethencourt, *Racisms: From the Crusades to the Twentieth Century* (Princeton, NJ: Princeton University Press, 2013), 280–83.

Such simplistic racist theories often associated "colors" with continents, red with the Americas, yellow with Asia, black with Africa, and white with Europe. The categorization was crude, inaccurate, and demeaning. It also legitimized the subjection by so-called whites of other regions of the world.

While race theorists imagined races as international, many also imagined national identity as being tied to those racial categories. In the new public schools, young students learned not only positive values of patriotic belonging, but also these racial hierarchies. Consider a textbook in the United States from 1896, *The Werner Introductory Geography*. Students reading this book learned that humans were divided into five races: white, yellow, black, red, and brown. "The white race," young readers learned, "is the one to which most people in our country belong and is the race most advanced in civilization ... The people of the white race are the most intelligent in the world."[25] Before they knew better, children learned that "whiteness" entailed superiority in intellect, proclivity to freedom, superior morality, and greater self-control. They also learned that being of another "color" meant being inherently inferior. As students reading a British textbook published in 1907 read, peoples in Africa were "extremely savage, practicing horrible forms of religion."[26] In the late nineteenth century, that is, students not only learned practical skills and patriotism; they also learned white supremacy. People also learned white supremacy in films, on radio, in museums, in public celebrations, and in newspapers. Some people challenged these stereotypes, but in the nineteenth century white supremacy became pervasive across the Americas and Western Europe.

It's critical to understand that the intensification of nationalism was inextricably linked to the spread of colonialism (which will be discussed in more detail in chapters 4 and 5).[27] After all, nationalism is both a positive identity defining what one is, as well as a negative identity of what one is not. Thus, nationalisms developing in Asia and Africa often developed an anticolonial flavor. Meanwhile, many forms of nationalism emerging in Western Europe and the Americas used white supremacy to justify colonial conquest, to limit immigration from supposedly nonwhite locations, and to assert racial hierarchies among residents of the nation-states.

By the end of the nineteenth century, racism, colonialism, and nationalism had become inextricably intertwined, though how and why this process took place varied by location. To get a sense of how this worked in Western Europe, consider a lecture by the noted statistician and biologist, Carl Pearson, given to

---

25. Horace S. Tarbell, *The Werner Introductory Geography* (New York: Werner School Book Company, 1896), 54.

26. A. J. Herberston, *The Junior Geography*, 2nd ed. (Oxford: Clarendon Press, 1907), 227.

27. See C. A. Bayly, *The Birth of the Modern World, 1780–1914: Global Connections and Comparisons* (Malden, MA: Blackwell, 2004).

members of Britain's Literary and Philosophical Society, meeting in Newcastle on November 19, 1900.

> I venture to assert, then, that the struggle for existence [in the United States] between white and red man, painful and even terrible as it was in its details, has given us a good far outbalancing its immediate evil. In place of the red man, contributing practically nothing to the work and thought of the world, we have a great nation ... The Australian nation is another case of a great civilization supplanting a lower race unable to work to the full the land and its resources ... The struggle means suffering, intense suffering, while it is in progress; but that struggle and that suffering have been the stages by which the white man has reached his present stage of development ... This dependence of progress on the survival of the fitter race ... is the fiery crucible out of which comes the finer metal.[28]

You may find Pearson's words troubling, but they demonstrate how explicitly many understood the connections between nationalism, colonial conquest, and racism by the turn of the twentieth century. They also give us a sense of the profound and misguided confidence felt by people who understood themselves to be "white." Finally, they show how some "white" people by the early 1900s justified the slaughter of entire civilizations as an expression of human progress.

But racial nationalists had a problem: despite their claims, nation-states were not—and have never been—ethnically, racially, or culturally unified. In order to rectify this, they worked to protect their nation-states' borders from racial impurities. We can find examples of new immigration laws that differentiated based on race, for example. From the 1880s, Argentina promoted immigration from Europe, based on white supremacist assumptions, but restricted the immigration of populations deemed barbarous, unhealthy, and inclined to crime.[29] In the United States, the Chinese Exclusion Act (1882) followed a similar logic. We see similar efforts in New Zealand, Australia, and Hawaii (before it was annexed by the United States in 1898).[30] There were also new efforts to purge supposed radical impurities within nation-states. One example comes from the increasing hostility to European Jews.[31]

---

28. Karl Pearson, *National Life from the Standpoint of Science* (London: Adam and Charles Black, 1901), 22–24.

29. Julia Rodriguez, *Civilizing Argentina: Science, Medicine and the Modern State* (Chapel Hill: University of North Carolina Press, 2006).

30. Adam McKeown, *Melancholy Order: Asian Migration and the Globalization of Borders* (New York: Columbia University Press, 2008).

31. Léon Poliakov, *The History of Anti-Semitism: Volume IV: Suicidal Europe, 1870–1933* (Philadelphia: University of Pennsylvania Press, 2003).

In 1879, the German Heinrich von Treitschke pronounced in a popular pamphlet titled *A Word about Our Jews* (*Ein Wort über unser Judenthum*) that Jews were a threat to the German nation itself. In France, Edouard Drumont published *Jewish France* (*La France juive*, 1886), a massive tome of virulent racial anti-Semitism that became an instant bestseller. Anti-Semitism spread in Britain and the United States during this period as well.

In the face of intensifying anti-Semitism, some Jewish Europeans came to feel that they should have their own nation-state. The most influential advocate for Jewish nationalism—called Zionism—was Theodor Herzl. A journalist from the Austro-Hungarian Empire, Herzl moved to Paris in 1891 to become a foreign correspondent for the newspaper, *New Free Press* (*Neue Freie Presse*). After witnessing the rising anti-Semitism in France, in 1896 Herzl published a book *The Jewish State* (*Der Judenstaat*), which proposed creating a nation-state for Jewish people.[32] The idea of the nation-state had become so powerful that minorities also started championing racialized, ethnic, and linguistic definitions of states as a solution to their hardships.

Multiethnic Empires during the Rise of Nation-States

In contrast to the Americas and Western Europe, by 1900 in the lands along (and across) the supposed Europe-Asia border, we don't find nation-states, but three multiethnic empires: the Austro-Hungarian Empire, the Russian Empire, and the Ottoman Empire (as seen in Map 3.1).[33] In each, we find a complex blend of peoples who spoke various (often multiple) languages and worshipped according to diverse religions, ruled by an imperial authority in Vienna, St. Petersburg, or Istanbul. Let's take a quick tour. The Austro-Hungarian Empire was a successor state of the Holy Roman Empire discussed in chapter 1.[34] The majority spoke German, but there were also significant speakers of Hungarian, Romani, Ukrainian, Yiddish, and at least eight Slavic languages. Religiously, the empire was an assortment of Roman Catholics, Protestants (of various stripes), Eastern Orthodox, Jews, and Sunni Muslims. In Austria-Hungary, strong multilingualism and weak ethnic allegiances meant that while nationalists were emerging, they had less success into the 1910s than their counterparts in France, the United States, or Argentina.[35]

---

32. This goal was achieved in 1947, and will be discussed in chapter 4.

33. In previous centuries, the extent to which these states fit within the idea of Europe described in chapter 1 varied.

34. The other main successor state was Germany, which united in 1871.

35. Pieter M. Judson, *Guardians of the Nation: Activists on the Language Frontiers of Imperial Austria* (Cambridge, MA: Harvard University Press, 2006).

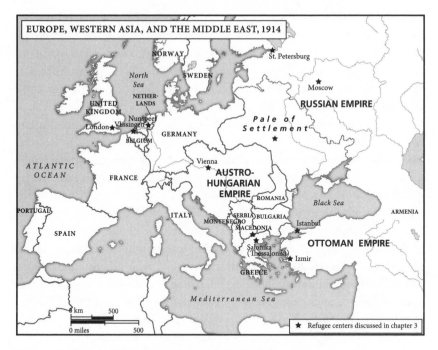

MAP 3.1 Europe, Western Asia, and the Middle East

Less than half of the Russian Empire was ethnically Russian.[36] The empire had large numbers of ethnic Ukrainians, Poles, Germans, Finns, Georgians, Armenians, and many others. By 1880, the largest Jewish population in the world—over five million—lived in Russia. Most of those were restricted to a region called the Pale of Settlement, including lands that today are in Poland, Belarus, Ukraine, and Lithuania. Internal developments that promoted national integration—like public schooling—affected Russia too, but on a more limited scale than in Western Europe. Colonial expansion—mostly into Central Asia and Siberia—also promoted nationalism. Starting during the reign of Czar Alexander III (r. 1881–1894), the government promoted a policy called Russification, which entailed efforts to suppress ethnic minorities' languages and cultures in favor of Russian. In 1883, publications in Ukrainian were banned. In 1884, the teaching of Polish was severely restricted. In 1885, Armenian-language schools were replaced with Russian ones. In places with large Muslim populations, Russification entailed forced conversions to Orthodox Christianity. Because Russification was sudden and coercive, resistance movements emerged among Poles, Armenians,

---

36. J. N. Westwood, *Endurance and Endeavour: Russian History, 1812–1992*, 4th ed. (Oxford: Oxford University Press, 1993), 92–94, 171, 84–88.

Latvians, and others. Russification extended to supporting, and even helping organize, mass attacks on Jews. The first of these so-called pogroms followed the assassination of Czar Alexander II in March 1881, sparked by rumors that one of the killers—a woman named Gesya Gelfman—was Jewish. More pogroms erupted in 1903–1906. Over a million Russian Jews fled to the United States between 1800 and 1900. Others moved to Latin America and Ottoman-controlled Palestine.

While ruled by ethnic Turks, the Ottoman Empire had large populations of Arabs, Greeks, Bulgarians, Romanians, Serbs, Kurds, Armenians, and others. Religiously, besides the majority Sunni Muslims, there were large populations of Christians (Roman Catholics, Eastern Orthodox, Armenians, and Protestants) and Jews. Ethnic and religious coexistence was the norm. One man in a later interview remembered that in the 1890s Muslims and Christians, Turks and Bulgarians coexisted fairly peacefully, visiting each other and exchanging gifts on holidays.[37] Tensions existed but ethnic diversity was not a leading source of societal conflict. Over the nineteenth century, Ottoman sultans attempted to centralize imperial authority, including improving infrastructure and professionalizing schooling and armies but, as in Russia, these efforts were more limited than in Western Europe.[38]

These three neighboring empires hotly competed for resources and influence. Situated between all three, the Balkans proved to be a political tinderbox. Most of the region was held by the Austro-Hungarian and Ottoman Empires, though Russia acted as the protector of Orthodox Christians and Slavic-speaking peoples in the region. Russia's interest in protecting Serbs and Bulgarians under Ottoman rule sparked the Russo-Turkish War of 1877–1878. Russia's victory forced the sudden creation of four new ethnically defined nation-states: Bulgaria, Serbia, Romania, and Montenegro (depicted on map 3.1) out of former Ottoman lands.[39] Yet because the ethnic, religious, and linguistic boundaries in this region were so fluid, there was no way to establish borders that would satisfy everyone. Romanian leaders resented that Russia took lands they felt belonged to them. Bulgarian leaders were angry they did not get Romania. The Serbian government felt it deserved Bosnia, which came under the control of Austria-Hungary. Historian Mark Mazower has shown that most individuals in the late nineteenth-century Balkans were uninterested in dividing up their communities by ethnicity.[40]

---

37. Donald Quataert, *The Ottoman Empire, 1700–1922* (Cambridge: Cambridge University Press, 2000), 174.

38. Mehrdad Kia, *The Ottoman Empire* (Westport, CT: Greenwood Press, 2008), 116–17.

39. Another new state, Eastern Rumelia, united with Bulgaria in 1885.

40. Mark Mazower, *The Balkans: A Short History* (New York: Modern Library, 2000).

However, the treaty ending the war unintentionally established a framework for competition for power using ethnic and linguistic arguments.

To see how this worked, let's take the example of the ethnically and religiously mixed region of Macedonia. After the Russo-Turkish War, the governments of Bulgaria, Serbia, and Greece each claimed this former Ottoman territory.[41] Bulgarian politicians hired specialists to prove their linguistic ties to Macedonians. Serbian leaders hired their own linguists, and added anthropologists who argued that they were more like Macedonians because they shared a ritual tradition called *slava*. The Greek government claimed Macedonia for itself, since it had historically fallen under the Greek Orthodox Church's authority and had been the birthplace of the ancient Greek leader, Alexander the Great. These arguments may have been genuine, but we can see how the sudden formation of ethnic nation-states created immediate political incentives to invent traditions. Initially, most Macedonians were indifferent to the matter. As one local reported to a French visitor, "Our fathers were Greeks and none mentioned the Bulgarians ... If we have to be Serbs, no problem. But for now, it is better for us to be Bulgarians."[42] Over time, however, competition for territory proved destabilizing. Bulgarian, Serbian, and Greek organizations paid for schools and churches and even hired armed thugs to promote their state's interests in Macedonia. By the 1890s, the question of how to define national belonging was proving dangerously volatile. In October 1912, Serbia, Bulgaria, and Greece put aside their differences to form an alliance that declared war on the Ottoman Empire. The outcome of this Balkan War was the division of Macedonia.[43]

The Refugee Crises of World War I

The Balkan War of 1912–1913 was not the last time debates about which people belonged to which Balkan states led to war. Only a year later, on June 28, 1914, activists who wanted Bosnia to join a separate Slavic state assassinated the heir to the Austro-Hungarian throne. The Austro-Hungarian military response provoked Russia to act to protect fellow Slavs. Germany joined its ally Austria-Hungary and then declared war on France, which had an alliance with Russia. On August 3, Germany invaded Belgium on the way to France, prompting the British government to declare war on Germany and Austria-Hungary. By the end of the year the Ottomans, who resented British and French imperialism in

---

41. Charles Jelavich and Barbara Jelavich, *The Establishment of the Balkan National States, 1804–1920* (Seattle: University of Washington Press, 1977), 208.

42. Quoted in Mazower, *The Balkans*, 99.

43. Disagreement about the division led to a second Balkan War the following year.

North Africa, allied with Germany and Austria-Hungary. Because major combatants also commanded vast empires across Africa and/or Asia, the war quickly became global. We'll learn more about the war's impact in Africa and Asia in later chapters, though the most intense fighting was in Europe. Equipped with new technologies such as machine guns, tanks, and poison gas, armies wrecked devastation on military and civilian populations. The Great War—or World War I as we call it today—also sparked the largest wartime refugee crisis ever seen.

There is no way to adequately cover the carnage caused by World War I here, or even to summarize the experiences of the roughly eighteen million displaced peoples. One and a half million ethnic Germans living in Russia flooded to Austria and Germany, fearing violence from Slavs. Half a million ethnic Italians in Austria-Hungary fled to Italy fearing violence from ethnic Germans. Hundreds of thousands of Serbians scattered across the Balkans after the Austro-Hungarian army invaded. Over 600,000 Armenians in the Ottoman Empire faced mass deportation to the province of Syria after the government suspected them of colluding with Russia. The forced expulsion led to a mass slaughter that most historians today refer to as the Armenian Genocide. Those who survived scattered for safety from Ottoman government-sponsored violence. In short, the war turned life upside down for millions of refugees, who fled with no time to pack, no route, and no maps.

For the period during the war, it is instructive to compare refugees moving between the nation-states of Western Europe and those moving within the multiethnic empires to the east. For an example of the first, consider the exodus of Belgian refugees who fled German occupation starting in August 1914, like those depicted in Figure 3.1. A couple hundred thousand each went to Britain and France, but the largest number—over a million people—fled to the Netherlands.[44] One refugee camp—in typically Dutch fashion—was a converted flower greenhouse at Gouda. Most camps were reasonably hospitable and included churches, schools, clinics, and even sports clubs. One exception, in a town called Nunspeet, was reserved for people the Dutch government viewed as "dangerous" or "less desirable," including those deemed to be delinquents, criminals, prostitutes, or potential spies. An English aid worker who visited the camp described it as operating under "quasi-military discipline."[45]

In Russia, the number of displaced people, like those depicted in Figure 3.2, reached well over three million within the first year of the war. The Russian army decided to slow the German advance by destroying entire towns as it withdrew.

44. Peter Gatrell, *The Making of the Modern Refugee* (Oxford: Oxford University Press, 2013), 33–34.

45. A. Ruth Fry, *A Quaker Adventure, The Story of Nine Years' Relief and Reconstructon* (New York: Frank-Maurice, 1927), 110.

FIGURE 3.1 Belgian refugees flee to the Netherlands, 1914.
Source: First World War Collection/Imperial War Museums

FIGURE 3.2 Refugees in the Russian countryside in November 1915.
Source: The German Federal Archives

The results were devastating. Those disproportionally affected were Jews and Poles, those living in the Baltics (Latvians, Lithuanians, Estonians, and ethnic Germans), as well as Muslim Tatars in eastern Ukraine. The Russian government also deported hundreds of thousands of Jews. Many refugees fled eastward into the Russian interior. New arrivals lived in railroad stations, schools, factories, movie theaters, army barracks, and monasteries—anywhere that could fit them! Alfred William Fortescue Knox, a British liaison officer with the Russian army, gives us a sense of the magnitude of the crisis: "Near Byselsk [i.e. Bel'sk, in eastern Russia] I passed twenty continuous miles of such fugitives. Some of them had come from as far as Plotsk [i.e. Płock, in Poland], and had been on the road a month . . . If asked where they were going, they replied that they did not know."[46] A Russian Red Cross worker reported passing at least 200,000 refugees along thirty miles of road.[47]

In some ways, the experiences of these two sets of refugees were similar. In both, families were fractured, and refugees were mostly older men, women, and children, in large part because so many adult men were in battle or dead. The aid worker Ruth Fry described three Belgian children from Antwerp—a brother, sister, and their cousin—who walked fifty-five miles over four days until they reached the Dutch city of Vlissingen, where the girl was taken in by the so-called *Home Belge*, which aided orphaned or abandoned girls (Fry gave no account of what happened to the boys).[48] Orphans overwhelmed charities in both cases. By the end of the war, 1.5 million children wandered around Russia without parents, many cold, sick, and hungry. Women often took leading roles in helping refugees. The British journalist Flora Luggard proved instrumental in founding the War Refugees Committee, which helped Belgian refugees in Britain. Wealthy Armenian women in Moscow organized fundraisers for refugees in Russia.[49] Women cared for orphaned children and widows. They also taught girls and young women "respectable" ways to earn a living, such as sowing and cooking, out of fear that they might otherwise be tempted to sell their bodies for sex.[50] In both crises, we find examples of sympathetic locals eager to help refugees but also of frightened xenophobes resentful of them.

---

46. Alfred William Fortescue Knox, *With the Russian Army, 1914–1917*, vol. 1 (London: Hutchinson & Co., 1921), 322–23.

47. Mariusz Korzeniowski, "Refugees from Polish Territories in Russia during the First World War," in *Europe on the Move: Refugees in the Era of the Great War*, ed. Peter Gatrell and Liubov Zhvanko (Manchester: Manchester University Press, 2017), 69.

48. Fry, *A Quaker Adventure*, 102.

49. Peter Gatrell, *A Whole Empire Walking: Refugees in Russia during World War I* (Bloomington: Indiana University Press, 1999), 77.

50. Gatrell, *Whole Empire Walking*, 120–21.

Locals often blamed refugees for driving up food prices and rents, taking local jobs, and spreading diseases. They also sometimes accused refugees of being traitors or spies.

One critical difference between the Belgian and Russian examples was how being a refugee affected national identities. The national integration of Belgium had followed the model described earlier for Western Europe, with an important exception: the country developed *two* official languages: Walloon (a dialect of French) and Flemish (a version of Dutch). Belgian nationalists existed, but so too did Walloon and Flemish nationalists. Ethnic nationalism was important to Belgian politics, but it was more splintered into diffuse camps than elsewhere in the West, in large part because the leading political parties—Catholic, liberal, and socialist—crossed the linguistic boundary. One might imagine that the shared experience of living as refugees might have galvanized nationalists from Belgium into a potent political force. But this was not the case for three reasons.[51] First, aid organizations did not distribute relief according to ethnicity or nationality. In the Netherlands, France, and Britain, organizations and governments delivered aid to refugees irrespective of ethnic identities. Second, many young Belgian refugees attended French, Dutch, and English schools, and sometimes embraced the host culture. Finally, when the refugees returned home after the war, they were not treated as martyrs for the nation, but as cowards and deserters who abandoned those who had suffered under German occupation. After the war, ethnic identities did not provide national solidarity in Belgian politics any more than they had before it.

In the Russian Empire, by contrast, the refugee crises of World War I galvanized nationalism among ethnic minorities. There were two main reasons for this. First, urban nationalists often proved eager to support refugees they perceived to be like them. Armenians in Moscow organized for Armenian refugees in the Caucuses, as they explained, "out of humanity and common national feeling."[52] Ethnically organized relief provided the main support too for Poles, Latvians, Lithuanians, Jews, and other groups forced to flee their homes.[53] Because of these efforts, aid recipients learned about people far away with whom they shared a common cause and culture. They also had strong incentives to identify with those groups, because it helped them secure desperately needed aid. Ethnic newspapers supported this process. The Armenian-language newspapers like *The Armenian Herald* (*Armianskii vestnik*) published stories of

---

51. Michaël Amara, "Belgian Refugees during the First World War (France, Britain, Netherlands)," in *Europe on the Move*, ed. Gatrell and Liubov, 197–214.

52. Gatrell, *Whole Empire Walking*, 67, 77.

53. Organizations serving these groups include the Polish Society for the Aid of War Victims, the Latvian Committee for Refugee Relief, the Lithuanian Central Relief Committee, and the Central Jewish Committee for the Relief of War Victims.

the plight of Armenian refugees.[54] The same was true of Latvian-, Polish-, and German-language newspapers and journals.[55] Journalists rarely offered dispassionate accounts, but instead promoted sympathies for ethnic and nationalist partisans. In short, the experiences of refugees connected educated nationalists with people who shared their language and culture, but had never been part of their "imagined community" before.

The second reason that Russia's refugee crisis promoted nationalism was that the government and local hosts categorized, provided aid to, and divided up refugees by ethnicity.[56] Hosts often treated refugees who spoke a specific language or dressed in a certain way as an undifferentiated bloc. Facing shared prejudices intensified a sense of common aggrievement. In the Russian Caucuses, Armenian refugees accused Kurds and Azerbaijanis of profiting from their hardship. In response to Russians confusing them with Germans (the Russians' enemy), Latvians adopted a more self-conscious and outward Latvian identity. The sudden shared adversity intensified feelings of ethnic nationalism.

Refugees in the Wake of World War I

In January 1919, diplomats met in Paris to write a settlement to the most gruesome war in world history. Europe was a complete wreck and its people traumatized. Death estimates vary, but run into the tens of millions. The negotiations were complex and tense. The settlement took years to implement and required multiple treaties. The most significant outcome of this diplomatic work was the promotion of the principle of national self-determination. On the face of it, the idea seems straightforward and virtuous. According to US President Woodrow Wilson, the goal was "that it be made safe for every peace-loving nation which, like our own, wishes to live its own life, determine its own institutions, be assured of justice and fair dealing by the other peoples of the world as against force and selfish aggression."[57] As we will see in later chapters, the new international order that developed after the war extended self-determination to many more Europeans, but not to peoples of Asia and Africa. But even for Europeans, there still existed no objective or unambiguous way to define who belonged to any given "nation."

---

54. Gatrell, *Whole Empire Walking*, 67.

55. Aldis Purs, "Working towards 'An Unforeseen Miracle' Redux: Latvian Refugees in Vladivostok, 1918–1920, and in Latvia, 1943–1944," *Contemporary European History* 16, no. 4 (2007): 284. Korzeniowski, "Refugees from Polish Territories." Ruth Leiserowitz, "Population Displacement in East Prussia during the First World War," in *Europe on the Move*, ed. Gatrell and Zhvanko, 23–44.

56. Gatrell, *Whole Empire Walking*, 143–44.

57. President Woodrow Wilson's Fourteen Points, January 8, 1918, http://avalon.law.yale. edu/20th_century/wilson14.asp.

Massive forced displacements of peoples resulted after the victorious powers chopped up the three multiethnic empires into new ethnic nation-states, including Turkey, Poland, Hungary, Finland, and Austria (see Map 3.2).[58] There were viable alternatives at that time.[59] One failed proposal, the Danube Federation, would have constituted a multiethnic state with a constitution that guaranteed rights and protected ethnic diversity. A mixed ethnic state like Belgium did provided a model for the creation of Czechoslovakia and the Kingdom of the Serbs, Croats, and Slovenes (later renamed Yugoslavia). Still, arguments in favor of creating ethnic nation-states mostly prevailed. The practical difficulties with turning multiethnic empires into ethnic nation-states were enormous. The first challenge was what the British politician George Curzon called at the time "the unmixing of peoples," that is, getting all people of a specific ethnicity into the state assigned to them. Ethnic minorities constituted 30 percent of the populations of the successor states. Six and a half million ethnic Germans lived within the new borders of Poland, Czechoslovakia, Italy, Hungary, and Romania. Over three million ethnic Hungarians lived in the states of Romania, Czechoslovakia, and Yugoslavia.

Massive displacements shocked a continent still reeling from war. Postwar Europe saw over 9.5 million refugees, some who fled voluntarily for their designated "homeland," some who fled fearing retaliation from ethnic majorities, some who faced governmental harassment, and some forced out in a population exchange. One might imagine that movements to people's new supposed "homelands" reflected their internalized senses of national belonging, but that does not capture the complexity of the situation. Ethnic Germans living in Poland fled in large numbers, but those living in Czechoslovakia mostly stayed put. In part, the difference is explained by worse economic conditions in Poland than Czechoslovakia, harsher treatment of ethnic Germans in the former lands of imperial Russia than in Austria-Hungary, and the fact that German-speaking communities in Czechoslovakia lived in more cohesive communities than those scattered across rural Poland.[60] Similarly, some 86 percent of ethnic Hungarians living outside of Hungary preferred to stay where they were. Most of those were peasants with little sense of patriotism and little interest in abandoning their farms for an uncertain future. Many ethnic Poles in postwar Germany were also happier to embrace German citizenship than to move to Poland.[61] In the former Austro-Hungarian Empire, bilingual people often chose their nationality

---

58. The Russian Empire collapsed in the face of famine and frustration with the war. The communists who took over the government formed the Union of the Soviet Socialist Republics in 1922. There too, separate republics were created along ethnic lines.

59. See the commentary from the Austrian jurist, Joseph Redlich, "Reconstruction in the Danube Countries," *Foreign Affairs* 1, no. 1 (1922): 73–85.

60. Brubaker, "Aftermaths" 195–200.

61. Hobsbawm, *Nations and Nationalism*, 134.

by where they could get the best aid packages.[62] More people were "citizens of convenience" than the logic of self-determination of nations could appreciate. Deciding who belonged to what nation was the result of complex negotiations, military clashes, and referenda. In 1920, a series of elections took place in border areas in which voters determined which nation their region would join. Once in place, the new governments promoted a sense of national belonging. That means that for many people in these former multiethnic empires nationalism was the *effect, not the cause* of the creation of nation-states that resulted from "unmixing."

The most carefully managed population transfer followed the Treaty of Lausanne (1923). According to that agreement, almost a half a million Muslim refugees moved from Greece to Turkey and three times that many Greeks left Turkey for Greece. The new League of Nations estimated that about a million Greeks died during the evacuations, mostly of typhus and starvation.[63] Ernest Hemmingway, the American journalist (and later famous novelist), reporting for the *Toronto Daily Star,* described twenty miles of Greek refugees fleeing the city of İzmir, "with exhausted, staggering men, women and children, blankets over their heads, walking blindedly along in the rain . . . It is all they can do to keep moving."[64] Refugees overwhelmed host communities. Salonika—the sixteenth-century refugee center in the Ottoman Empire described in chapter 1—received 160,000 refugees from Turkey.[65] Many refugees deeply resented "unmixing." A Muslim mufti forced to flee Greek-controlled Macedonia explained: "We, Muslims, will never accept this exchange, and we declare that we are pleased with our Greek government."[66] We get a similar sense from a newspaper report from *The Times* of London:

> Few, if any, of the Turks in Greece desire to leave, and most of them will resort to every possible expedient to avoid being sent away. A thousand Turks . . . have sent several deputations to the Greek Government, asking to be allowed to return . . . A few weeks ago a group of Turks from Crete came to Athens with a request that they be baptized into the Greek Church, and thus be entitled to consideration as Greeks![67]

---

62. Judson, *Guardians of the Nation*, 228.

63. Michael Marrus, *The Unwanted: European Refugees from the First World War Through the Cold War* (Philadelphia: Temple University Press, 2002), 96–106.

64. "A Silent, Ghostly Procession," in Seán Hemingway, ed. *Hemingway on War* (New York: Scribner Classics, 2003), 267.

65. Dimitri Pentzopoulos, *The Balkan Exchange of Minorities and its Impact upon Greece* (Paris: Mouton & Co., 1962), 97.

66. Bruce Clark, *Twice a Stranger: The Mass Expulsion that Forged Modern Greece and Turkey* (Cambridge, MA: Harvard University Press, 2006), 158.

67. "Greece and her Neighbours", *The Times* (London), Wednesday, December 5, 1923, p. 11.

The experience of the "unmixing" of Salonika (now mostly known by its Greek name Thessaloniki) also provides an example of how dividing cultures by ethnicity can intensify, rather than quell hostilities. Britain's consul to Salonika described how the experience radicalized some refugees:

> They arrive in Turkey with the memory of their slaughtered friends and relations fresh in their minds, they remember their own sufferings and persecutions ... they see no wrong in falling on the Greek Christians of Turkey and meting out to them the same treatment that they themselves have received from the Greek Christians of Macedonia.[68]

The idealistic plan to preserve peace through national self-determination thus unintentionally intensified ethnic hostilities.

People for whom no "homeland" could be identified exposed another glaring contradiction in the process of "unmixing." Hundreds of thousands of stateless people—mostly Armenians from the former Ottoman Empire and Jews from the former Russian Empire—had no designated homeland and thus faced the disturbing prospect that no nation would accept them. Over a million Armenians remained homeless in the wake of the Ottoman government's forced removals and mass killings in 1915. Many fled to the Russian-controlled Caucuses, while others settled as refugees in Egypt and Syria, like the woman and children in Figure 3.3.

FIGURE 3.3 Armenian refugees in post–World War I Syria.
Source: Library of Congress Prints and Photographs Division

---

68. Quoted in Mark Mazower, *Salonica, City of Ghosts: Christians, Muslims, and Jews 1430–1950* (London: HarperCollins, 2004), 338–39.

Hundreds of thousands wandered. In 1917, Russian revolutionaries pulled their country out of the war. Georgians, Azerbaijanis, and Armenians in the Caucuses briefly formed a multiethnic state, though the union fell apart in the face of an Ottoman advance.[69] In 1918–1919, 700,000 Armenians, who had never had an ethnically homogenous "homeland," now held a small, economically marginal state measuring only 4,500 square miles. That winter almost 30 percent of the population died of starvation, hypothermia, and typhus. Howard Heinz, the son of the famous Pittsburgh ketchup mogul, reported from his visit:

> There are 500,000 refugees who are in need of food . . . The lack of food is so serious that women actually go into the fields and obtain grass roots which they cook into a kind of broth and serve as boiled greens . . . The little children naturally get the worst of this situation because they cannot eat such material and it is among the children that the death rate is the highest . . . The people are clad in vermin-infested rags, with no possible change or chance of improvement, because there is no clothing of any kind or textile material available at any price.[70]

While President Wilson hoped that the United States would take over Armenia, the US Senate's refusal to accept the Paris Peace settlement made that plan impossible. Meanwhile, Britain and France focused on controlling the Ottoman Empire's former Arab lands (which we'll discuss in chapter 4), and took little interest in the plight of the Armenians.

According to a treaty signed in March 1921 between leaders of the new post-imperial states—Turkey and the Soviet Union—the Soviet Union incorporated the republic of Armenia while Turkey claimed all of Asia Minor. The Turkish government forcibly deported thousands of Armenians to Greece as part of the population exchange of 1923.[71] Another 225,000 Armenians became stateless. Eventually, many went to the Soviet Union or to former Ottoman provinces in the Arab world now under British or French control (The Mandate for Syria and Lebanon, Transjordan, and Mandatory Palestine, depicted in Map 3.2). At least 60,000 moved to France, while others went to the United States and Canada. Many Armenians in the diaspora began asserting their people's ancient connection to a specific homeland—they had become a nation without a state.

---

69. The Azerbaijanis allied with the Ottomans, while the Georgians provided oil to the Germans in exchange for military protections. The Armenians were on their own.

70. As quoted in James L. Barton, *Story of Near East Relief (1915–1930): An Interpretation* (New York: Macmillan, 1930), 123.

71. Marrus, *The Unwanted*, 104.

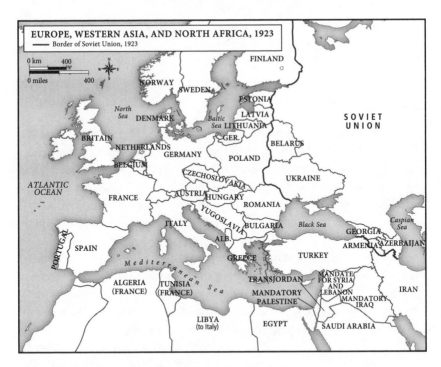

MAP 3.2 Europe, Western Asia, and North Africa, 1923

Hundreds of thousands of Jews became stateless as well. Once the war was over, there were over two thousand anti-Semitic attacks in the lands of the former Russian Empire, which killed over 30,000 Jews and left a half a million homeless. The largest number of postwar Jewish refugees found themselves in the newly created state of Poland. Others sought refuge in Ukraine, Germany, and Czechoslovakia. In Germany, 560,000 of these so-called Eastern Jews (*Ostjuden*) faced heightened anti-Semitism in the 1920s. An intensified Polish nationalism after the creation of Poland featured strong anti-Jewish sentiments as well.[72] Jewish soldiers who had volunteered to serve in the new Polish army were instead put into concentration camps. In 1920, Austria also expelled large numbers of Jewish refugees to Poland, which refused their entry. In 1923, Poland expelled refugees streaming back to their former homes from Russia. But Russia refused to take them back. The impoverished masses of stateless refugees were pushed back and forth, trapped in a new world of ethnic nation-states that offered no place for them. The United States—which had for decades served as a release valve for European migrants (including Russian Jews)—shut its borders to most war refugees in 1924. Britain encouraged Europe's stateless Jews to move to formerly Ottoman-ruled Palestine,

---

72. Marrus, *The Unwanted*, 63–65.

which was now under its colonial administration. That decision had consequences for Palestine (discussed in chapter 4), but the 37,000 Jews who moved there between 1919 and 1923 barely made a dent in the stateless crisis.

Conclusion

World War I, as no one imagined at the time, only served as prelude to World War II. Once again conflicts centered on the proper borders of Europe's ethnic nation-states. Once again a regional conflict turned into a global war within weeks. Once again armies used ever more advanced technologies to kill on an unprecedented scale. Once again Europe's Jews suffered disproportionally. And once again some people resorted to massive forced population displacements and genocide to try to enact their belief that peace would come with ethnic homogeneity. There is not space here to describe the takeover of the German government by Adolf Hitler's National Socialist (Nazi) Party, the outbreak of war, the Holocaust, or the refugee crisis that followed. But it's useful to offer a general comparison to understand just how important the emergence of ethnic nation-states between the 1880s and the 1910s proved in shaping refugee crises of the twentieth century.

Much had changed between the start of World War I and the start of World War II. Most notably, unlike in the Balkan crises, the Nazi party that controlled Germany from 1933 to 1945 promoted a version of ethnic German nationalism that saw racial impurity as a threat to the very existence of the German nation, inspired by late nineteenth-century scientific racism described earlier. This worldview justified Germany's annexation of Austria in March 1938 and its capturing of an ethnic German enclave from Czechoslovakia that October. It also justified the boycotts on Jewish-owned business in 1933, depriving Jews of citizenship, and banning intermarriage of Jews with gentiles. Characteristic of Hitler's ethno-racial nationalism was his commitment to the idea that superior races naturally defeat and replace inferior ones, similar to the claims made by Carl Pearson at Britain's Literary and Philosophical Society in 1900. Like Pearson, Hitler saw the extermination of supposedly inferior races as the necessary expression of progress and the natural order. Hitler's "final solution" to the supposed problem of ethnic diversity, usually called the Holocaust (in Hebrew, *Shoah*), entailed the mass execution of about six million Jews, as well as other perceived enemies of the German nation. The year 1939 was different from 1914 in other ways too. A global and devastating economic depression now intensified people's fears and anxieties. International socialism—the most widespread alternative to the West's nationalism and imperialism—was now at the head of one of Europe's Great Powers. Fears of communism only fueled the popularity of hypernationalist fascists.

Many more people died in the Second World War than in the first—approximately 60 million compared to around 18 million. Many more also experienced life as a war refugee. Estimates suggests that as many as 60 million Europeans were displaced during World War II.[73] Millions of forced laborers and prisoners of war returned home. Millions more fled the Soviet army as it imposed order in postwar Russia. Ethnic Germans living outside of Germany faced mass expulsions as well. There were also larger numbers of stateless people, now called "displaced persons," sitting in camps or wandering aimless. Many of these were Jewish survivors of the concentration camps.[74] At the time, the refugee crises facing Europe after 1945 seemed unprecedented. In terms of its scope, it was. But the refugee crises of World War II drew on much of the same logic as the refugee crises of World War I. At its core, that logic assumed that people who shared a language and ethnicity naturally belonged to a nation-state, which had rights to self-determination, a geographical homeland, and sovereignty over its affairs. World peace and political order, Western thinkers widely agreed, depended on having nation-states as the global political norm. Anomalies—stateless and colonized peoples—were problems to be solved, whether by nation building or by migration. What distinguished Germany's Third Reich was not that its leaders disagreed with this consensus, but that they proved willing to promote genocide to acheve an ethnically-defined nation-state.

This chapter began with the Rudyard Kipling's joke about patriotism. At the crux of his attempt at humor in 1902 was the poet's acknowledgment that homelands are mere contrivances, alongside his admission that he still loves his best. Kipling wrote at a time when nationalism seemed exciting, before two world wars had tarnished that optimism. By 1943, Hannah Arendt, a German Jewish refugee from the Nazi government, made a similar point, but this time with deadly seriousness:

> Some day somebody will write the true story of this Jewish emigration from Germany; and he will have to start with a description of that Mr. Cohn from Berlin who had already been a 150% German, a German super-patriot. In 1933 that Mr. Cohn found refuge in Prague and very quickly became a convinced Czech patriot—as true and as loyal a Czech patriot as he had been a German one. Time went on and about 1937 the Czech Government, already under some Nazi pressure, began to expel its Jewish refugees ... Our Mr. Cohn then went to Vienna; to adjust oneself there a definite Austrian patriotism was required. The German invasion forced Mr. Cohn out of that country. He arrived in ... France. Therefore, he prepared his adjustment to the French nation by identifying himself with "our" ancestor Vercingetorix.[75]

---

73. Gerard Daniel Cohen, *In War's Wake: Europe's Displaced Persons in the Postwar Order* (Oxford: Oxford University Press, 2012).

74. Angelika Königseder and Juliane Wetzel, *Waiting for Hope: Jewish Displaced Persons in Post-World War II Germany*, trans. John A. Broadwin (Evanston, IL: Northwestern University Press, 2001).

75. Hannah Arendt, "We Refugees," in *Altogether Elsewhere: Writers on Exile*, ed. Marc Robinson (Boston: Faber & Faber, 1994), 116. Vercingetorix was a French national hero revered for leading the Gauls against Roman invasion in the first century BCE.

Arendt wrote her essay, "We Refugees," ten years after escaping Germany, following a path not dissimilar from her character Mr. Cohn, but ending in New York City. Arendt pointed out that when citizenship, rights, and human dignity are recognized and protected exclusively by nation-states, two dangers lurk. First, totalitarian regimes can use the logic of nations to justify extreme violence in the name of national sovereignty and self-determination. Second, people whom no states accept lack protection—they become abandoned by their fellow humans.

Refugees like Arendt had watched the optimistic inclusiveness of national belonging descend into two devastating world wars. In the years that followed, world leaders took actions that forever changed the history of refugees. First, they agreed to recognize *human rights* guaranteed to every living person, regardless of citizenship status. Second, the new United Nations (established in 1945) set international rules for the treatment and protection of refugees. Finally, they began the gradual process of dismantling Europe's colonial regimes and helping create new independent nation-states with self-determination and sovereignty of their own. As they attempted to re-draw the world map and protect universal human rights, however, they also inadvertently promoted new waves of refugee crises, which we will turn to in chapter 4.

FURTHER READING

Anderson, Benedict. *Imagined Communities: Reflections on the Origin and Spread of Nationalism.* London: Verso, 1991.

Evans, Richard. *The Pursuit of Power: Europe, 1815–1914.* New York: Penguin, 2016.

Gatrell, Peter. *A Whole Empire Walking: Refugees in Russia during World War I.* Bloomington: Indiana University Press, 1999.

Gatrell, Peter, and Liubov Zhvanko, eds. *Europe on the Move: Refugees in the Era of the Great War.* Manchester: Manchester University Press, 2017.

Hobsbawm, E. J. *Nations and Nationalism since 1780: Programme, Myth, Reality.* Cambridge: Cambridge University Press, 1990.

Marrus, Michael. *The Unwanted: European Refugees from the First World War Through the Cold War.* Philadelphia: Temple University Press, 2002.

Purseigle, Pierre. "'A Wave on to Our Shores': The Exile and Resettlement of Refugees from the Western Front, 1914–1918." *Contemporary European History* 16, no. 4 (2007): 427–44.

4   SELF-DETERMINATION, DECOLONIZATION, AND ASIA'S POSTWAR REFUGEE CRISES

> Imagination fails to picture, the wild delirium of joy with which he [US President Woodrow Wilson] would have been welcomed in Asiatic capitals. It would have been as though one of the great teachers of humanity, Christ or Buddha, had come back to his home, crowned with the glory that the centuries had brought him since he last walked the earth.[1]

These are the words of V. S. Srinivasa Sastri, a schoolteacher and activist against British rule of India, written a few years after the end of World War I. You probably have heard of Woodrow Wilson (I mentioned him in chapter 3, after all). You may even be familiar with some of his achievements. But I doubt that you'd be willing to equate him with the likes of Jesus or Buddha! Yet Sastri's claim is central to this chapter. In the previous chapter, we learned that the principle of national self-determination offered a way of reorganizing Europe after World War I. In this chapter, we'll learn that this idea also changed the world.

---

1. V. S. Srinivasa Sastri, *Woodrow Wilson's Message for Eastern Nations* (Calcutta: Association Press, 1925), preface.

Across Asia, telegraphs brought news of Wilson's speeches to newspapers in Arabic, Hindi, Korean, Vietnamese, and many other languages. After reading his words, anticolonial activists living in colonies across Asia travelled to the peace talks taking place in Paris. In speeches and petitions, they echoed Wilson's lofty rhetoric. These delegates were not naïve followers of American idealism, but educated elites who found in Wilson's arguments about national self-determination the best opportunity yet to end colonial rule. As it turns out, they failed. Colonialism largely continued as it had.[2]

A generation later, however, decolonization took hold across Asia (but not Africa, the subject of chapter 5). Given what we know about Europe and America, it's worth reflecting on what Asia is as a "big idea." In chapter 1 we learned that Asia was originally a term used by ancient Greeks to describe lands to their east, as opposed to "Europe" to their west. A helpful term to understand Asia further is the word "Orient." The word derives from the Latin word for "east" (*oriens*), which ancient Romans used the same way that ancient Greeks used "Asia." Later, when the metageography of Europe presented that peninsula as geologically distinct from Asia (or the Orient), Europeans also imagined themselves as culturally distinct from Asians. During the nineteenth century, "Orient" came to take on additional meanings. In the context of expanding European global imperialism, Europeans lumped together a vast array cultures as different as Arabic-speaking Muslims, Bengali-speaking Hindus, Vietnamese-speaking Buddhists, and Korean-speaking Confucians as "Orientals." Europeans often imagined "Orientals" as timeless, backward, seductive and in need of European guidance and governance.[3] Like the idea of America, the metageography of the Orient (which used to be a synonym for Asia) came to justify European colonialization of Asia.

This chapter focuses on what happened when three European colonies in Asia gained independence. In each case, the way colonial subjects had developed ideas of nationalism and self-determination in Asia also helps us understand massive refugee crises that took place in the late 1940s. We begin with Israel/ Palestine, because it connects to topics discussed in the previous chapter: stateless Jews and the "unmixing of peoples" in the former Ottoman Empire. New competing forms of nationalism adopted by various Arab residents of British-ruled Mandatory Palestine and Jewish immigrants by the 1920s and 1930s go a long way to explaining the Palestinian refugee crisis of 1948. The second case, India/Pakistan, offers a chance to see how colonialism pitted different groups

---

2. For this point, see Erez Manela, *The Wilsonian Moment: Self-Determination and the International Origins of Anticolonial Nationalism* (Oxford: Oxford University Press, 2007).

3. Zachary Lockman, *Contending Visions of the Middle East: The History and Politics of Orientalism*, 2nd ed. (Cambridge: Cambridge University Press, 2010), 66–99.

of indigenous colonial subjects against one another in ways that contributed to another massive refugee crisis associated with decolonization in Asia. We will end by reflecting briefly on Japanese decolonization of Korea, which provides a useful reminder that imperialism could be non-Western as well. All three refugee crises point to the period of 1945–1950 as a destabilizing moment in the history of Asia.

The Emergence of Nationalisms in Colonial Palestine

For four centuries (1516–1919), the Ottoman Empire both *did* and *did not* rule over Palestine. What do I mean by that? I mean that the term "Palestine" (originally a province of the Roman Empire) only referred to an unspecified region in the Ottoman Empire that actually spanned two sanjaks (districts), Beirut and Jerusalem. Most people there spoke Arabic, though many were multilingual. Religiously, most were Sunni Muslims, but there were many Shi'ite Muslims, Christians (mostly Greek Orthodox) and Jews (many of whose ancestors had immigrated as refugees, described in chapter 1). For centuries, Muslims, Christians, and Jews coexisted in Palestine, including having friendships, and even sharing religious festivals (like the Muslim Nebi Musa, Christian Easter, and Jewish Purim). As elsewhere (though to a lesser extent) nineteenth-century Palestinians became connected through new technologies, such as railroads and steamships, but also newspapers. Most Palestinian newspapers did not promote ethno-nationalism but celebrated what historian Michelle Campos calls "civic Ottomanism," a sense of shared purpose, equality, and respect among the empire's ethnic and religious groups.[4] We should be careful not to idealize this coexistence. Economic resentments festered between the rural poor and wealthier urbanites. Further, Sunni Muslims held a privileged relationship to the state, which frustrated some Jews and Christians. Still, politics and social relations proved relatively stable through the nineteenth century. If we are looking for the origins of an entrenched divide that helps us understand the Palestinian refugee crisis, we will not find it in some supposedly timeless struggle between religions or ethnicities.

Changes around the turn of the twentieth century transformed Ottoman Palestine. Jewish refugees fleeing anti-Semitism in Russia (described in chapter 3) arrived in significant numbers. Many of these migrants embraced a form of religious Zionism. Turning to their sacred texts for comfort, religious Zionists emphasized that God had promised a specific homeland—"the Land of Israel"—to his chosen people. That is, religious Zionists merged an ancient idea of a

---

4. Michelle U. Campos, *Ottoman Brothers: Muslims, Christians, and Jews in Early Twentieth-Century Palestine* (Stanford, CA: Stanford University Press, 2011), 1–19.

"promised land" with the newer idea of the "nation-state." Supporters of civic Ottomanism resented the newly arriving religious Zionists. Between 1908 and 1914, more than six hundred anti-Zionist articles appeared in Arabic-language newspapers. This hostility convinced many local Jews to abandon civic Ottomanism in favor of Zionism. At the same time, some religious minorities feared that the Muslim-dominated government might never treat them as equals, despite promises of increased equalities.[5] Finally, truncation of the Empire (also discussed in chapter 3) also increased the equation among government officials of the Ottoman identity (a political idea) and the Turkish identity (an ethnic or linguistic idea). In the Arab-speaking parts of the empire, this process encouraged a renaissance of Arabic identity. A form of Arab nationalism even started to appear in the 1910s. However, its chief proponent, Naguib Azoury, found scant support in Palestine, where civic Ottomanism remained strong.[6] These new tensions were real, but far from existential threats. When World War I broke out, more pressing challenges dominated.

It's worth pausing to add a note about World War I and Palestine. A key reason the Ottomans sided with Germany and Austria-Hungary related to the Suez Canal. Opened in 1869 by the British, the canal allowed steamships to travel from the Mediterranean to the Red Sea, dramatically shortening the journey from Europe to colonies in Asia. However, there was a snag: the canal was in Egypt, which was an Ottoman tribute state. In order to ensure its control of Suez, Britain worked to replace the Ottomans in Egypt. By 1882, the British government achieved de facto success. But if the Ottomans hoped to stem the tide of losses by allying with Germany and Austria-Hungary, their defeat had the opposite effect; after World War I, the Allies dismantled the Ottoman Empire.

After the war, inspired by the international community's new principle of national self-determination, anticolonial activists from across Asia composed petitions and speeches for the Paris Peace Conference, using Wilson's rhetoric.[7] For the Arab-speaking lands, the most important speaker was Emir Faisal I, a former Ottoman elite from a distinguished family in Mecca.[8] On January 29, 1919, he proposed that a new Arab nation should be ruled by his father. "I base my request," Faisal explained, "on the principles enunciated by President Wilson ... and am confident that the Powers will attach more importance to the bodies

---

5. Rashid Khalidi, *Palestinian Identity: The Construction of Modern National Consciousness* (New York: Columbia University Press, 2010), 119–44.

6. Campos, *Ottoman Brothers*, 237.

7. Manela, *The Wilsonian Moment*.

8. See N. Masalha, "Faisal's Pan-Arabism 1921–33," *Middle Eastern Studies* 27, no. 4 (1991): 679–93.

and souls of the Arabic-speaking peoples than to their own material interests."[9] About Palestine, Faisal explained:

> The Jews are very close to the Arabs in blood, and there is no conflict of character between the two races. In principles we are absolutely one. Nevertheless, the Arabs cannot risk assuming responsibility of holding level the sides of the clash of races and religious that have, in this one province, so often involved the world in difficulties.[10]

Let's take a minute to reflect on Faisal's words. First, Faisal claimed that Arabic-speaking people made up a nation, and not Palestinians (or any other regional group). This forced Faisal to perform verbal jumping jacks when discussing Palestinian Jews: Jews were one people with Arabs "in principles," he claimed, though he refused to take responsibility for clashes between the two. Faisal's seeming contradiction makes more sense if we remember that his goal was to convince Western diplomats to appoint his father to rule over a large independent state made up of all lands with Arabic-speaking majorities, not to describe historical reality. But Faisal's proposal had to contend with an alternative. A group of pro-Zionist delegates led by Chaim Weizmann argued that Palestine should instead be set aside for a Jewish nation-state.[11]

Neither Faisal nor Weizmann got his way. At Paris, world leaders chopped up much of the former Ottoman Empire into British and French colonies, including Syria and Lebanon, Iraq, and Palestine (shown in Map 4.1). Europeans did not entirely ignore the principle of self-determination, however. Rather, they invented a new kind of colony, called a "mandate." What distinguished a mandate from other colonies? In terms of political, economic, and social relations, not much. The key difference was that Europeans recognized their rule over these new colonies, "until such time as they were able to stand alone."[12] That is, the mandate system offered what earlier colonial systems did not: the *promise of future national sovereignty*, if colonized peoples could demonstrate to their colonizers that they had the characteristics of a "modern nation." While the mandatory powers never made any plans

---

9. David Hunter Miller, ed. *My Diary at the Conference of Paris, with Documents*, vol. 4 (New York: Appeal Press, 1924), 30. By "material interests" Faisal likely alluded to the Suez Canal. Oil, for which Arabia is famous today, was only discovered there three year later.

10. Miller, ed., *My Diary*, 298–99.

11. See Weismann's *Statement of the Zionist Organization regarding Palestine* at https://unite-apps.un.org/dpa/dpr/unispal.nsf/9a798adbf322aff38525617b006d88d7/2d1c045fbc3f126 88525704b006f29cc.

12. Article 22 of the Covenant of the League of Nations, http://avalon.law.yale.edu/20th_century/leagcov.asp.

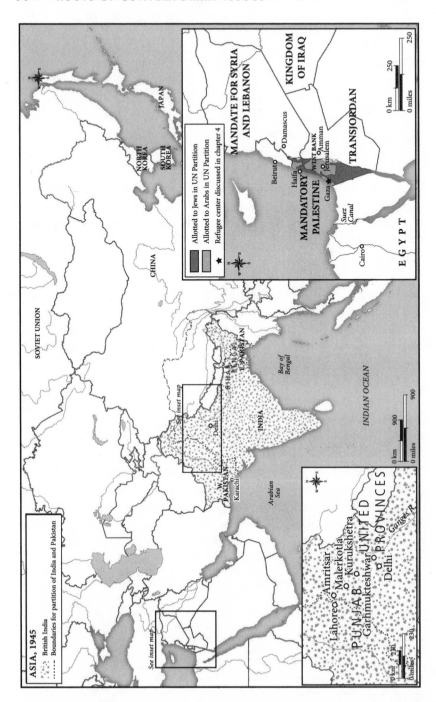

MAP 4.1 Asia, 1945

to give up their colonies, the mandate system created a powerful incentive for anti-colonialists to embrace nationalism. And that is just what they did.

Since the British government had declared its support for a Jewish homeland, Zionists expected Jews would soon gain national self-determination in Palestine. In the face of intensifying anti-Semitism, brutal pogroms, and many Jews' experiences of wandering stateless after World War I, Britain's position offered hope to the hopeless, and a nation to the nation-less. And so, European Jews continued moving to Mandatory Palestine. They called this move *aliyah* (Hebrew for "ascension"), a biblical reference (2 Chronicles 36:23) that referred to the return of the Jewish people to "the Land of Israel" after almost two millennia of diaspora.

In the 1920s, Arabic-speaking Muslims and Christians in Palestine resented the *aliyah* for what they perceived as its undermining of their way of life. Arab Palestinians sometimes called the immigrants "Moscovites"—casting doubt onto the immigrants' identities, categorizing them as another group of foreign Europeans out to subjugate non-Europeans.[13] In the 1920s, Muslim and Christian Arabic speakers in Mandatory Palestine also started using the term "Palestinian" to refer to themselves as a nation.[14] Some Arabs also assaulted Zionist immigrants. For their part, many Zionist immigrants understood the hostility they faced within a long narrative of Jewish suffering. Following a series of Arab attacks on Zionist settlers in 1920–1921, one Jewish newspaper ran the headline "Will Jerusalem Become Like Kishinev [a Russian pogrom of 1903–1905]"?[15] Meanwhile, Zionists disregarded Palestinian nationalism because they believed that Palestinians were merely a subset of the larger Arab world.

Two episodes of violence upped the ante. First, hostilities erupted in August 1929, sparked by tensions about a site that Jews called the Wailing Wall—a surviving section of the Second Temple in Jerusalem, whose destruction by the Roman Empire in 70 CE marked the start of nearly two millennia of diaspora. Muslims viewed the site as a part of the Noble Sanctuary (*al-Haram al-Sharif*), the location from which they believed Muhammed ascended to heaven in 621 CE. The site had been shared for centuries, but in the summer of 1929, tensions about access to it exploded. Rioting Palestinian Arabs killed 133 Jews. Dehumanizing rhetoric on both sides increased. Arabs used militant language like "Palestine is our land and the Jews our dogs." Jews referred to Arabs as "packs of wolves from Arabia" and "desert savages."[16] After a crackdown by British authorities—killing 166 Arabs—many Palestinian nationalists grew to believe that only militant action would help

---

13. Anita Shapira, *Land and Power: The Zionist Resort to Force, 1881–1948*, trans. William Templer (Oxford: Oxford University Press, 1992), 68.

14. Khalidi, *Palestinian Identity*, 145–75.

15. Quoted in Shapira, *Land and Power*, 111.

16. Shapira, *Land and Power*, 174, 99.

them achieve self-determination. Meanwhile, many Jews feared that they would remain insecure so long as they remained a minority in Palestine. Violence again erupted in 1936, following demonstrations by Palestinians against British rule and Jewish immigration. These attacks convinced the British government in July 1937 to propose dividing Mandatory Palestine into two states—one Arab and one Jewish—and to relocate residents to the appropriate territory, following the model of the Greek–Turkish population exchange of 1923 (discussed in chapter 3). While Jews were divided about the plan, most Palestinian Arabs resented the idea of handing over Palestinian land. Riots broke out, resulting in more violence, more resentments, and ever-stronger Palestinian nationalism. In 1939 the British floated a new proposal to establish an independent state that Arabs and Jews would jointly rule.

At this point, events taking place in Europe intervened. In Germany the hypernationalist and anti-Semitic Nazi party had taken control of the government in 1933. In 1938 a pogrom against German Jews by paramilitary forces and civilians marked the start of a slide toward genocide. After the Nazi invasion of Poland in 1939, the government organized death squads whose job included pushing Jews out so that Germans could move in. By 1941 the Nazi government starting forcibly sending Jews in massive numbers to concentration camps, where they were worked to the point of exhaustion and often death.[17] German officials also performed mass executions in industrial-scale extermination facilities. By the time that Allied forces defeated Germany in 1945, the Nazi government had killed roughly six million Jews and five million other so-called undesirables. For many, the Holocaust re-raised the question introduced by Theodor Herzl in 1896: Should Jews have their own nation-state?

On November 29, 1947, the newly established United Nations answered this question by passing a proposal to transform Mandatory Palestine into two nation-states—one Jewish and one Arab. According to the plan, Jews (then 32 percent of the population) would get 55 percent of the territory, majority Arabs would receive 40 percent, and the area around Jerusalem and Bethlehem would remain under international control. It's hard to overstate the anxiety felt by Jews in Palestine at this moment. Trauma of the attempted genocide of their people combined with fear about the hatred and violence they faced from Arabs. The fact that militant Palestinians had recruited Muslims in Bosnia to serve the Nazis only reinforced a narrative that linked the Holocaust and Palestinians.[18] Many Jews saw *every* Palestinian Arab as an inherent threat, while many Palestinian Arabs saw *every* Jewish settler as an inherent threat. This logic contributed to an extremely volatile situation.

---

17. Léon Poliakov, *Harvest of Hate: The Nazi Program for the Destruction of the Jews of Europe* (Syracuse, NY: Syracuse University Press, 1954).

18. Jeffrey Herf, "Nazi Germany's Propaganda Aimed at Arabs and Muslims during World War II and the Holocaust: Old Themes, New Archival Findings," *Central European History* 42, no. 4 (2009): 709–36.

Refugee Crisis in Israel/Palestine

The announcement of the partition plan ignited both a war and a refugee crisis. Starting in December 1947, a spiral of reciprocal violence transformed into all-out war. On May 14, 1948, the victorious Jewish side proclaimed the new nation-state of Israel. The following day, armies of neighboring Arab states invaded. By the end of the year, however, Israeli forces had secured most of the former lands of Mandatory Palestine. In retrospect, the quick and decisive Israeli victory does not seem surprising. Israelis had better financial backing and superior military training than the poorer, more rural Palestinians, who were also deeply divided among themselves.[19] Decisions made by external actors also worked in Israel's favor. The United Nations put an embargo on selling weapons to either side. When Arab forces ran out of ammunition in July 1948, their military was crippled. But private arms dealers in Czechoslovakia sold Israel weapons, in contravention of international law.[20] Meanwhile, the British withdrew their troops even as the fighting was happening.[21]

Much of the violence was cyclical and retaliatory. In Haifa, after a Jewish militia killed six and wounded fifty Arabs, a group of Palestinians responded by bombing a gathering of Jews, killing thirty-nine and injuring eleven. Jewish paramilitaries retaliated by raiding a series of Palestinian villages and killing adult males they suspected of sedition.[22] Palestinians faced far higher causalities, intense bombing, sieges, and mass detentions. Palestinian morale and social order collapsed. Shops, hospitals, and public transportation all closed. The Palestinian Christian Arab Khalil al-Sakakini wrote in his diary about what he saw in Jerusalem that spring:

> Since midnight yesterday the Jews are strongly attacking our neighbour-hood . . . The shells from their guns, the bullets . . . In this situation, what wonder that the inhabitants think of moving to another neighbourhood or another city . . . many . . . have migrated to the Old City [of Jerusalem], to Beit Jala [in what became the West Bank], to Amman [in Jordan], to Egypt and elsewhere.[23]

---

19. Rashid Khalidi, "The Palestinians and 1948: The Underlying Causes of Failure," in *The War for Palestine*, ed. Eugene Rogan and Avi Shlaim (Cambridge: Cambridge University Press, 2007), 12–36.

20. Arnold Krammer, *The Forgotten Friendship: Israel and the Soviet Bloc, 1947–53* (Urbana: University of Illinois Press, 1974), 76–80.

21. Ellen Jenny Ravndal, "Exit Britain: British Withdrawal from the Palestine Mandate in the Early Cold War, 1947–1948," *Diplomacy & Statecraft* 21, no. 3 (2010): 416–33.

22. Benny Morris, *The Birth of the Palestinian Refugee Problem Revisited* (Cambridge: Cambridge University Press, 2004), 101.

23. Quoted in Morris, *Birth*, 124.

Palestinians of means were the first to flee, but by the spring of 1948 the migration had turned into a deluge. Considerable debate emerged about how and why they fled.[24] Palestinians argued—and some still argue—that the mass departure was the result of a premeditated Jewish effort at ethnic cleansing.[25] Jews argued—and some still argue—that Palestinians voluntarily abandoned their homes. "The simplest, most human explanation," suggested one British reporter at the time, "is that the Arabs have fled out of pure disorder."[26] While Palestinians and Jews blamed each other, the foreign correspondent put the blame on an abstraction—disorder—sidestepping the question of responsibility. Part of the challenge in resolving this debate is that witnesses offered contradictory testimonies and the victors destroyed many records. Another problem was that the fast-changing nature of these events contributed to confusion and chaos. There is more consensus today than there once was, however. Few scholars claim that the mass removal was intentionally orchestrated, while most agree that Jewish forces played an active role in removing Palestinians. The historian Alon Confino tells the tale of what happened in the Arab-dominated town of Tantura, about thirteen miles south of Haifa. Jewish militias emptied the village, rounding up all adult men, while relocating women, children, and the elderly.[27] The militias' actions were improvised, not premeditated, as Palestinians later claimed. But the Palestinians did not move voluntarily, as Israelis later insisted. The Jewish militiamen demanded that women sign a declaration that they were leaving of their free will (though some refused). Many refugees wept as they were shipped off, ultimately to the neighboring state of Jordan.

Something like three quarters of a million Palestinians fled or were forcibly removed between April and August of 1948. About 200,000—including the children in the port city of Jaffa depicted in Figure 4.1—escaped or were forced into two enclaves within the lands of former Mandatory Palestine, the West Bank (which fell under Jordanian rule), and the Gaza Strip (governed by Egypt). The rest crowded into refugee camps in the neighboring states

---

24. For an overview see Steven Glazer, "The Palestinian Exodus in 1948," *Journal of Palestine Studies* 9, no. 4 (1980): 96–118.

25. For example, see Ilan Pappé, *The Ethnic Cleansing of Palestine* (Oxford: Oneworld Publications, 2006). The historian Benny Morris critiqued this work in *The New Republic*, March 16, 2011, in a review titled "The Liar as Hero," https://newrepublic.com/article/85344/ilan-pappe-sloppy-dishonest-historian.

26. "Mass of Refugees on the Move: A New Problem," *The Times* of London, April 24, 1948, p. 4.

27. Alon Confino, "Miracles and Snow in Palestine and Israel: Tantura, A History of 1948," *Israel Studies* 17, no. 2 (2012): 25–61.

FIGURE 4.1 Hundreds of thousands of Palestinians were forced from their homes in 1948, including these children fleeing Jaffa.
Source: United Nations

of Jordan, Syria, Lebanon, and Egypt. An American observer reported in December 1948:

> Gaza is an unattractive little Arab town with an original population of about 25,000. It now has, in addition, about 60,000 refugees. They pack sidewalks, take up the vacant lots and the public market, occupy barnyards, and generally seem to fill in every empty space which the town might have had. They live in churches, mosques, schools, and public buildings.[28]

The Palestinian refugee crisis was the first to receive humanitarian relief from the new United Nations International Refugee Organization (IRO). Some aid workers expressed frustration when victims starved because they did not fit a bureaucratic definition of a "refugee."[29] The IRO also faced enormous problems trying to keep track of people in this unsettled and dynamic situation. Refugees often failed to report deaths in their family so that they did not have to give up the deceased's

---

28. Quoted in Morris, *Birth*, 467.

29. Ilana Feldman, "Difficult Distinctions: Refugee Law, Humanitarian Practice, and Political Identification in Gaza," *Cultural Anthropology* 22, no. 11 (2007): 138–39.

rations. Friends also passed around newborns, each claiming it was theirs, so that they could add to their food allotment.[30] Initially, Palestinian refugees hoped that they might return to the Palestinian state that had been promised by the United Nations, while Israeli Jews hoped that the refugees would quietly assimilate into Arabic-speaking host societies. Neither happened. Instead, Palestinians remembered the exodus as *al-Nakbah* (Arabic for "catastrophe")—their status as victims dispossessed of their homeland became central to Palestinian national identity.

At the same time, Jewish leaders faced the immediate question of where to settle the new immigrants moving to Israel from post–Holocaust Europe. Already on February 17, 1948, the Israeli government presented a plan for building Jewish settlements on recently emptied Arab land. By August 1949, 135 new communities had been established.[31] Between 1948 and 1951, nearly 700,000 Jews immigrated to Israel. Many of these had been displaced persons during and after World War II, but others came from Arab-majority states like Iraq, where anti-Jewish feelings skyrocketed. By 1949 it seemed clear to most everyone involved that Palestinian refugees would not simply return: too many Arab villages had been destroyed during the war or bulldozed afterward and too many Jews—many of whom were former refugees with their own heartbreaking stories—had resettled in these lands.

The Palestinian refugee crisis of 1948–1950 helped create the conditions that led to an even larger refugee crisis in 1967. We will not discuss that topic here, in part because it follows much of the same logic—competing calls for national self-determination combined with spiraling retaliatory violence. Today there are over five million Palestinian refugees. Most have known no life except as a refugee, either in overcrowded camps in Gaza and the West Bank, usually called the Occupied Territories, or in slums outside major Arab cities. The tragedy of the Israel/Palestine conflict is that two competing identities are deeply rooted in senses of victimhood based on events that took place during the 1940s. Most historical accounts have treated the conflict as rooted in its specific *location on the planet*—a sacred land for three world religions. But as we shall see, it is also useful to see its cause traced back to a specific *moment in world history*. Turning to the example of the refugee crisis in India and Pakistan—which took place at almost the same moment, can help explain what I mean.

The Emergence of Nationalisms in Colonial India

As with Palestine, what we mean by "India" can be a bit confusing. Originally the term referred to a region along the Indus River. From 1858 to 1947, "India"

---

30. As reported by the Annual Report of the Director of the UNRWO for the Palestinian Refugees in the Near East, July 1, 1951 to June 30, 1952, A/2171, unispal.un.org.

31. Morris, *Birth*, 376–77.

referred to a British colony in that region of Asia (depicted in Map 4.1). Most people there speak one of many Indo-Aryan languages, including Hindi, but also Bengali, Gujarati, Punjabi, and others.[32] Religiously, besides the majority Hindus, Muslims, Christians, Sikhs, Jains, Buddhists, and Zoroastrians have lived in the region for centuries. The term Hinduism—Europeans first introduced the suffix "-ism" in 1830—is hardly satisfactory since the Hindu tradition is not defined by a set of doctrines or devotion to any exclusive prophet or deity.[33] Most Hindus accept a diversity of gods and believe that when a body dies, its soul is reborn in another body (which need not be human), adopting a new set of ethical duties (dharma) each time. In 1526, a Turkic military commander, Zahir al-Din Muhammad, conquered large swaths of India and established the so-called Mughal Empire, the most powerful state in the region for centuries.[34] While the number of Muslims increased under Mughal rule, Hindus remained the majority. There were conflicts and even wars during the Mughal period, but Hindu–Muslim animosities were not central to these tensions.

Rather, Hindu–Muslim divisions emerged as the unintended consequences of British imperialism. The first Englishmen arrived in the early 1600s as merchants working for the East India Company (EIC).[35] In 1759, the EIC secured from the Mughal emperor the right to administer taxes and finances for Bengal. While the EIC professed obedience to the emperor, in practice, Bengal functioned as a lucrative colony for the company. Into the 1800s, the EIC extended its authority into southern India and the Ganges River Valley and established plantations where Indian workers produced cotton, jute, and other raw materials that were shipped to Britain for processing. The British also invested in the kinds of massive infrastructure projects that we saw in Europe in chapter 3—railroads, canals, a postal service, and telegraph lines—which facilitated government coordination and made it easier to suppress dissent.

The most dramatic and consequential act of anticolonial resistance in EIC-ruled India came with the Indian Rebellion of 1857–1858. The revolt started with a mutiny of disgruntled Bengali soldiers, which inspired angry landlords, nobles, and peasants to take up arms against British rule. No coherent ideology, leadership, or strategy characterized the rebellion, except perhaps resentment of colonialism. Rebels attacked British soldiers, officers, merchants, and their

---

32. In the south, people speak a variety of Dravidian languages.

33. Gavin Flood, *An Introduction to Hinduism* (Cambridge: Cambridge University Press, 1996). See also M. V. Nadkarni, "Is Caste System Intrinsic to Hinduism? Demolishing a Myth," *Economic and Political Weekly* 38, no. 45 (2003): 4783–93.

34. John F. Richards, *The Mughal Empire* (Cambridge: Cambridge University Press, 1993).

35. For an introduction, see Ian J. Barrow, *The East India Company, 1600–1858: A Short History with Documents* (Indianapolis: Hackett Publishing Company, 2017).

families, but also burned administration buildings, army barracks, and banks to the ground. British troops brutally suppressed the rebellion. But now colonial officials understood the danger of losing control of their colony, which generated much of Britain's skyrocketing wealth. The British crown took direct control of India from the despised EIC. After 1869, the Suez Canal allowed the government to intensify its rule by more quickly moving troops, personnel, and equipment between Britain and India.

In the following decades, many Hindus grew defensive of violations of their sacred traditions, which encouraged them to embrace "invented traditions," in a similar fashion as was happening at the same time in Europe and the Americas (discussed in chapter 3). One influential development was the spread of cow veneration. Many (but not all) Hindus had long embraced vegetarianism as a way of expressing *ahimsa* (nonviolence), a Hindu principle of avoiding harm to other forms of life. Some ancient Hindu texts emphasized the importance of cows in particular, though their messages were inconsistent.[36] A much stricter emphasis on the veneration of cows as sacred began among a group of Sikhs—members of a monotheist religion that had its heartland in the Punjab region. Later a Hindu movement called Arya Samaj (founded in 1875) emphasized the infallible authority of sacred texts called the Vedas, some of which stressed the sacrality of cows. By the 1880s cow protection societies were being founded all over India. The connection of Hindu revivalism and intensification of cow protectionism inadvertently provoked hostilities with Muslims. In the 1890s, cow protectors filed lawsuits against butchers, most of whom were Muslim, in part because many Hindus felt that killing animals for meat violated *ahimsa* and in part because Muslims only ate meat that had been prepared according to their sacred traditions. Muslim butchers resented condemnations from cow protectors. In 1893, a series of deadly Muslim–Hindu riots broke out—provoked by the hatreds that had developed over cow protectionism. Telegraphs and newspapers quickly brought news of the violence to Hindus across India, further intensifying devotion to cow protection and stoking anti-Muslim views.[37] Because many Hindu advocates of Indian self-rule framed anticolonialism as a defense of sacred Hindu traditions, that is, they unexpectedly promoted Hindu–Muslim hostilities.

By the late nineteenth century, anticolonialist calls for some measure of autonomy in India became powerful, though few advocated an outright break from Britain. The most influential self-rule organization, the Indian National Congress (INC, founded in 1885), only presented itself as the "loyal opposition." While

---

36. D. N. Jha, *The Myth of the Holy Cow* (London: Verso, 2002).

37. Barbara Metcalf and Thomas Metcalf, *A Concise History of Modern India*, 2nd ed. (Cambridge: Cambridge University Press, 2006), 153–54.

most INC members were Hindus, the organization welcomed Muslims and other religious minorities. Still, many of its leaders rooted their anticolonialism in Hindu concepts. Bipin Chandra Pal (1858–1932), for instance, put the Hindu concept of *swaraj* (also sometimes spelled svaraj) at the center of his nationalism. As he wrote in 1910: "Not self-government ... but SVARÂJ was proclaimed as the new ideal ... The term is used in the Vedânta [i.e., knowledge coming from the Veda texts] to indicate the highest spiritual state, wherein the individual ... is established in perfect harmony with all else in the world ... svarâj—fully represents the spirit of Indian Nationalism."[38] Basing Indian nationalism on Hindu principles spoke to the beliefs of peoples who were otherwise divided by language and culture. But it also alienated some Muslims. In 1906 a group of educated Muslims formed the All-India Muslim League, which opposed British colonialism, but also promoted Muslim interests.

Politics in India became polarized between supporters of the INC and the Muslim League in the run up to World War I. Some Hindu nationalists acted in defense of an idea they called "Hindustan." Defenders of the Muslim League feared Hindu tyranny unless there were protections to ensure that Muslims had a say in politics. By accepting this argument, the British colonial government only further pitted Hindus and Muslims against one another and established the precedent that only Muslims could represent Muslims.

All sides in India supported Britain in World War I, including over a million soldiers who fought in Africa and Europe. When the war was over, Indians were inspired by Woodrow Wilson's vision that self-determination of nations would promote peace and security. In 1918, one Indian nationalist wrote that "It is impossible that the noble truths uttered by President Wilson in his War Message, could be limited in their application. Henceforth, his words are going to be the war cry of all small and subject and oppressed nationalities in the world."[39] The INC named Mohandas Gandhi, Bal Gangadhar Tilak, and Syed Hasad Iman to attend the Paris Peace Conference. In preparation, Tilak published a pamphlet with an illustration showing an imaginary steamship, the *S.S. Self-Determination*, heading on its journey "from autocracy to freedom," depicted in Figure 4.2. Passengers boarding represented Turkey, Israel, China, Arabia, and others. The ship's captain, Woodrow Wilson, asked whether India—represented by a woman wearing a sari—was coming along. The passport officer, British Prime Minister Lloyd George, explains that she cannot come because she does not have

---

38. Bipin Chandra Pal, *The Spirit of Indian Nationalism* (London: Hind Nationalist Agency, 1910), printed in Elie Kedourie, ed. *Nationalism in Asia and Africa* (London: Frank Cass, 1970), 351.

39. Lala Lajput Rai, "India and the World War," *Young India* 1, no. 2 (1918): 2–3. On Lajput Rai, see Manela, *Wilsonian Moment*, 85–90.

FIGURE 4.2 Woodrow Wilson as the captain of the ship *S.S. Self-Determination*, in Bal Gangadhar Tilak, *Self-Determination for India* (London: Indian Home Rule League, 1919).
Source: Library of Congress

a passport. Tilak's purpose was to point out British hypocrisy in only promoting self-determination when it proved economically convenient.

Advocates for Indian independence were deeply disappointed with the Paris Peace Conference: India would remain a British colony. But as with the mandate system in Palestine, hints emerged that future independence might be possible. Western powers granted India membership in the new League of Nations, though Britain controlled its votes. The Government of India Act of 1919 also created a so-called diarchy—shared governance in provincial administration. The British gave India "training wheels" for autonomy, which could be taken off once Indians reached some unnamed stage of development. This prospect only spurred on Indian nationalism. The anger and frustration felt by Indian anticolonialists was worsened by a massacre of anticolonial protestors on April 13, 1919, while the Paris Peace Conference was still meeting.

These disappointments convinced the INC to adopt a fervent hostility to colonial rule. The leading figure in that transition was Mohandas Gandhi

(1869–1948). In 1920 Gandhi pointed out that the British only ruled India with the complicity of the Indians:

> It is as amazing as it is humiliating that less than one hundred thousand white men would be able to rule three hundred and fifteen million Indians. They do so somewhat undoubtedly by force but more by securing our cooperation in a thousand ways ... they want India's manpower for their imperialistic greed. If we refuse to supply them with men and money, we achieve our goal, *Swaraj*, equality, manliness.[40]

Gandhi also appealed to the Hindu principle of *ahimsa* to argue that violence would only worsen the situation. Peaceful noncompliance, he urged, offered a superior tool to collapse British authority than violence. Like *swaraj*, *ahimsa* offered a guiding principle that was indigenous to India, making it a useful focus for nationalist unity. Gandhi also used mass media—especially newspapers and radio—to spread his message. In 1921, he stopped wearing Western suits and donned the clothes of a South Asian peasant. The move proved to be a propaganda coup; across India and around the world, Gandhi symbolized a principled alternative to Western norms of thinking. True independence, Gandhi argued, required not just self-rule, but a transformation of self and society—a rejection of Western values, which he believed were rooted in an obsession with the empty accumulation of material goods. For Gandhi, Britain's vast wealth and political power symbolized its weakness, not its strength. In the 1920s and 1930s, Gandhi and his allies staged massive marches and boycotts, and engaged in peaceful civil disobedience that forced concessions from the British government and earned worldwide attention.

While Gandhi believed Indian national unity required Hindus and Muslims to cooperate, some Muslims continued to feel marginalized by the Hindu majority. The most powerful Muslim voice was Muhammad Ali Jinnah (1876–1948), who served as leader of the Muslim League from 1913. Jinnah argued that Muslim autonomy required freedom from British rule, but also freedom from Hindu domination. At the Muslim League's annual convention, on March 22, 1940, Jinnah explained that it was a fantasy, "that the Hindus and Muslims can ever evolve a common nationality ... Hindus and Muslims belong to two different religious philosophies, social customs and literatures." It would be a mistake, he added, to "yoke together two such nations under a single state."[41] In the early 1940s, Jinnah's Muslim League rapidly signed up some two million new members.

---

40. Louis Fischer, ed., *The Essential Gandhi: An Anthology* (New York: Vintage Books, 1963), 158.

41. Printed in Jamil-ud-din Ahmad, ed. *Some Recent Speeches and Writings of Mr. Jinnah* (Lahore: Sh. Muhammad Ashraf, 1942), 153.

During this same period, Muslims began rallying around the term "Pakistan." The word had been coined by a Punjabi student at Cambridge University, Chaudhry Rahmat Ali, who wrote a pamphlet titled "Now or Never: Are We to Live or Perish For Ever?"[42] Ali made up the term by using initials for the regions of India with large Muslim populations: (P) Punjab, (A) Afghanistan (aka North-West Frontier Province), (K) Kashmir, (S) Sindh, and (TAN) Baluchistan. The new word stood for a belief that Muslims should govern themselves.[43] In a way, it served as a counterpoint to the Hindu term *swaraj*.

Shortly after Germany's surrender in World War II, a mixture of economic hardship and anticolonialist protests convinced the British government to announce its withdrawal from India.[44] National elections for the new state took place in late 1945 and early 1946. Campaigning proved tense. Muslim Leaguers advocated for a separate Muslim state, with "Pakistan" as their motto. Members of the INC promoted a multireligious, multiethnic state united by pan-Indian nationalism, using *swaraj* as a rallying cry.[45] Politicians made wartime metaphors, equating their opponents with Nazis and demanding noble sacrifices. Both groups viewed any vote for the other side as a violation of decency.[46] Anxiety was in the air. Gandhi's spirit of nonviolence and Hindu–Muslim cooperation was losing out to a climate of fear and suspicion. As a friend from the Muslim League leadership wrote to Jinnah on March 1, 1946, "At present one must shout with the crowd or get lynched by the crowd, and the feeling has been created that one who is not a Leaguer . . . should be hanged like a dog forthwith."[47] As in Palestine, that is, people deployed dehumanizing language to describe their opponents.

In the spring of 1946, diplomatic negotiations quickly started up on what the new independent state would look like. Amazingly, after the vitriol of the recent election, by May delegates had hammered out a deal to keep a united India with some autonomy devolved to Muslim-majority regions. Everyone sighed a breath of relief. But optimism was short-lived. Reservations on both sides required

---

42. Chaudhry Rahmat Ali, "Now or Never: Are We to Live or Perish Forever," (Cambridge: The Pakistan National Movement, 1933), http://www.columbia.edu/itc/mealac/pritchett/00islamlinks/txt_rahmatali_1933.html.

43. David Gilmartin, "Partition, Pakistan, and South Asian History," *Journal of Asian Studies* 57, no. 40 (1998): 1081–83.

44. See press coverage in "Steps Towards Indian Self-Government." *The Times* of London, September 20, 1945, p. 4.

45. Yasmin Khan, *The Great Partition: The Making of India and Pakistan*, New ed. (New Haven, CT: Yale University Press, 2017), 30–39.

46. Khalid Bin Sayeed, *Pakistan: The Formative Phase* (Oxford: Oxford University Press, 1968), 203–04. Mushirul Hasan, *India Partitioned: The Other Face of Freedom* (Delhi: Lotus Collection, 1995), 45.

47. Quoted in Khan, *Great Partition*, 53.

delegates to reconvene in June. This second round of talks collapsed under the weight of mutual suspicions. The British government resolved that it would simply divide the country into two separate nation-states after all.

Refugee Crisis in India/Pakistan

As soon as this decision was made, violence broke out. The first attacks came from Muslims fearing that they would be targeted by Hindus. On August 16, 1946, some Muslim Leaguers in Calcutta (Bengal's capital, today known as Kolkata) staged a protest. Shouting slogans like "Larke Lenge Pakistan" (we shall win Pakistan by force), the protestors attacked a group of Hindus.[48] Over the next four days, Calcutta erupted in violence. Rioters smashed and burned buildings and killed opponents in the streets. Estimates suggest that roughly 4,000 people were killed, 10,000 injured, and another 10,000 fled. In Noakhali district (also in Bengal) Muslims who heard about attacks on their coreligionists in Calcutta assaulted Hindus. The violence spread to some 350 villages. About 50,000 mostly Hindu refugees fled for safety. Across the country, Hindus read harrowing newspaper reports of looting, rapes, the desecrations of Hindu temples, and Muslims slaughtering cows and forcing Hindus to eat beef. Many Hindus retaliated. By the third week of October, Hindus in Bihar province—north of Bengal—attacked Muslims, even destroying entire Muslim villages to get revenge. Some 5,000 to 10,000 people were killed, while over 120,000 Muslims fled. Hindu retaliatory violence took place at Garhmukteshwar (in the United Provinces, today the state of Uttar Pradesh) in early November. According to anti-Hindu propaganda, the violence was horrific; pregnant women were disemboweled, babies' heads slammed into walls, genitalia and limbs chopped off, and corpses and the heads of the dead displayed in public.[49] Muslims responded with retaliatory killings of their own.

The violence convinced British politicians to speed up the partition to August 15, 1947. They assigned two commissions to draw boundaries for the new nation-states. Meanwhile, bureaucrats quickly split the government's property in two, with 80 percent going to India and 20 percent to Pakistan (roughly matching the population divide). Teams divided up tables, chairs, stationary, weapons—everything that was needed to run a government. Bureaucrats and soldiers could choose which nation-state they would serve. Some 25,000 officials in India started relocating to Karachi, the new capital of Pakistan. By August, cartographers had created two borders across 3,800 miles (depicted on Map 4.1). In the east, a line ran

---

48. Ian Talbot and Gurharpal Singh, *The Partition of India* (Cambridge: Cambridge University Press, 2009), 69.

49. Talbot and Singh, *The Partition of India*, 67.

between India and the Muslim-majority portion of Bengal, which was named "East Pakistan." To the west, the boundary between India and "West Pakistan" mostly followed preexisting borders between Muslim-majority and Hindu-majority provinces, except that in the north it cut through religiously mixed Punjab. East Pakistan and West Pakistan were to be administered by a single government.

Even before the announcement of the new border, violence exploded worse than before. The worst hostilities erupted in Punjab. Not only was it the only province to be broken up, but over half of its districts were contested. Punjab was also the homeland to India's Sikhs, who feared they would face ethnic cleansing if they found themselves living in a state defined by its commitment to Islam. Violence exploded in early March 1947. In Amritsar (today in India) and nearby Lahore (today in Pakistan) Muslims attacked Hindus and Sikhs, hoping to take over the two cities. Violence rippled out from there, with Muslim gangs burning entire Hindu and Sikh towns before their rivals could act. Tens of thousands— mostly Sikhs—fled to refugee camps in Hindu-dominated areas. When they could regroup, Sikh and Hindu militias too went on killing sprees to reclaim lost lands. Militias of all three religious groups raided villages, destroyed buildings, and attacked railcars filled with escaping passengers. Often the attackers described themselves as brave soldiers for their homeland, honorable protectors of freedom, and heroes willing to face martyrdom for justice.

Violence against women took on special importance. Crowds of young men— Hindu, Sikh, and Muslim like—used rape as a weapon and a tool to dishonor and shame female victims, their families, and their entire community.[50] Attackers sometimes branded rape victim's breasts or faces with slogans like "Long Live Pakistan" (*Pakistan Zindabad*) or "Victory to India" (*Jai Hind*). Afterward, many victims faced a life of shame and dishonor. Often their families would not take them back. Many women were forced into homelessness or prostitution. Some faced the prospect of converting and marrying their rapist. Women who were impregnated as a result of rape often tried to induce miscarriages or give themselves risky abortions. Other victims committed suicide. This sexual violence only provoked more retaliations.

The whole subcontinent did not see violence. Malerkotla, a Muslim princely state in Punjab with a mixed population, remained peaceful. In 1997, the novelist Khushwant Singh recalled tranquility in his wealthy suburb of Lahore. During the worst of the violence, he wrote, the well-to-do "went about in our cars to our offices, spent evenings playing tennis . . . [and] had dinner parties where Scotch . . . flowed like waters of the [River] Ravi [which runs past Lahore]."[51] Further,

---

50. Pippa Virdee, "Negotiating the Past: Journey through Muslim Women's Experience of Partition and Resettlement in Pakistan," *Cultural and Social History* 6, no. 4 (2009): 467–84.

51. "Last Days in Lahore," in *Outlook*, May 28, 1997, https://www.outlookindia.com/magazine/story/last-days-in-lahore/203610.

there are plenty of testimonies of mercy and compassion. One Hindu man later wrote, "I feel honour-bound to record that the lives of my children and those of about six hundred educated Hindus and Sikhs … were saved by the efforts of some God-fearing Muslims who gave them shelter in their houses, even at the risk of their lives."[52]

Initially the new governments tried to stop the mass migrations of people fleeing the violence. By August 1947, after it was clear that approach was unrealistic, both started coordinating what became probably the largest population transfer in world history. Sikhs and Hindus living in the new state of Pakistan fled to India, while Muslims in India escaped to East or West Pakistan. The numbers were astounding. During the last week of October 1947 alone, over 570,000 Muslim refugees fled to Pakistan via the crossings at Amritsar and nearby Ferozepur. Khushwant Singh (mentioned earlier) described trains crowded with refugees in the newly divided Punjab in his 1956 novel, *Train to Pakistan*:

> From the roof, legs dangled down the sides onto the doors and windows. The doors and windows were jammed with heads and arms. There were people on buffers between the bogies [the connecting links between the cars] … The engine driver started blowing the whistle and continued blowing till he had passed the Mano Majra station [on the border]. It was an expression of relief that they were out of Pakistan and into India.[53]

As many as fifteen to twenty million people were displaced during the partition.

In some cases, people walked in caravans of thirty to forty thousand. As they moved, people died of starvation, exhaustion, and cholera. Dust storms hit and walkers without shoes developed terrible sores on their feet. The American photographer Margaret Bourke-White, who gained fame photographing Nazi concentration camps, recorded these journeys. Bourke-White's photos, like the one in Figure 4.3, offered compelling testimony to the drama of the refugee crisis. Refugees interviewed later remembered taking only what they could carry with them in the caravans plodding across the countryside.[54] In some cases, husbands and fathers left first, to find a new home for the family. In other cases, wives and mothers left first with their children, while husbands stayed behind to keep an income or to sell their house. After families separated, reconnection proved

---

52. Khan, *Great Partition*, 139.

53. Khushwant Singh, *Train to Pakistan* (Westport, CT: Greenwood Press, 1975), 43–44.

54. Urvashi Butalia, *The Other Side of Silence: Voices from the Partition of India* (Durham, NC: Duke University Press, 2000), 80.

FIGURE 4.3 Partition refugees, photograph by, Margaret Bourke-White.
Source: The LIFE Collection

enormously difficult, either because family members died or could not be located, or because border crossings had closed.

To provide a more concrete sense of how the refugee crisis played out, it's
useful to focus on the two capital cities—Delhi and Karachi. About a third of
Delhi's population was Muslim. On August 14–15, 1947 Hindu gangs killed
some 20,000 Muslims in the streets. The Indian government established camps
where Muslims could be protected (or monitored, depending on one's perspective) until they moved to Pakistan. The largest camp—located in a sixteenth-
century Mughal fort called Purana Qila—filled with 50,000 refugees within days
of opening.[55] Morale was abysmal: residents had lost their homes, lived in squa-
lor, and prepared for an unwanted transfer to a faraway place with an uncertain
future. In all, some 330,000 Muslims fled Delhi during the chaos. Meanwhile,
between August and October of 1947 over 320,000 Hindus and Sikhs flooded
into Delhi. The government had little time to prepare a response. One answer,
developed by the Ministry of Relief and Rehabilitation, was to allow new arrivals
to move into the houses that Muslims had just emptied.[56] Many Hindu and Sikh

55. Vazira Fazila-Yacoobali Zamindar, *The Long Partition and the Making of Modern South
Asia: Refugees, Boundaries, Histories* (New York: Columbia University Press, 2007), 34.

56. Zamindar, *Long Partition*, 28–29.

refugees arrived with bitter anti-Muslim resentments. As a result, many Muslims who initially had opted to stay felt threatened, and chose instead to flee.

Before Partition, Karachi had been a sleepy port city and capital of Sindh province. While Sindh was mostly Muslim, about half of Karachi's residents were Hindus, many of whom were professionals and civil servants. The city avoided the vicious violence seen elsewhere, but became a major destination for Muslim refugees. Some newcomers were government and military personnel who chose to serve the Pakistani government. Others were Muslim refugees fearful that Hindu tyranny would overcome India. Still others fled violence perpetrated by Hindu and Sikh gangs. Pakistanis referred to new arrivals as *mohajir*, a term of Arabic origin that refers to the prophet Mohammad's flight from Mecca in 622 CE that marks the start of the Islamic calendar. This choice of words suggested that escaping to Pakistan constituted an act of submission to God's will. Karachi's population tripled, even as the new national government still operated out of tents. Many newcomers arrived simmering with anger toward Hindus and Sikhs. Karachi's Hindus and Sikhs fled for India as quickly as they could. In a fitting mirror of what happened at Delhi, the Pakistani government allowed mohajirs to move into recently abandoned houses in Karachi.

One difference between the two states was that Pakistan was incapable of handling an influx of tens of millions of Muslims from India. Pakistanis also feared that India would use the partition as a pretext to rid itself of impoverished and destitute Muslims. As a result, both the Pakistani government and ordinary Pakistanis hoped to limit the number of Muslims streaming in. Many mohajirs felt disappointed by such an unenthusiastic reception. They rioted when they did not feel welcomed or could not find housing. Their anger grew deeper after the government tried to convince some to return to India. While most mohajirs stayed, by March 1948, Indian officials claimed that some one thousand Muslims per day were returning to India, disillusioned with the promise of "Pakistan."[57] Hindu and Sikh refugees who had taken over their homes in India frantically urged the government not to welcome Muslims back. Many Hindu nationalists also questioned whether Muslims who had initially opted for Pakistan could ever be trusted in India. The Indian government put increasing restrictions on Muslims who returned to India after first going to Pakistan. Pakistan followed suit. As a result, many thousands of people bounced around as stateless for years.

Hundreds of refugee camps on both sides of the border housed millions of refugees. Some of these were state-sponsored, but others were improvised encampments, where refugees took over schools, temples, mosques, or government buildings. The largest camp in India, in the city of Kurukshetra, housed over a quarter-million refugees. Sometimes as many as 25,000 refugees arrived in the middle of the night at the Kurukshetra camp, leaving staff scrambling.[58] Health

57. Zamindar, *Long Partition*, 86.

58. Khan, *Great Partition*, 163.

conditions in the camps were horrible: cholera, dysentery, and smallpox proliferated. Social workers did their best to provide inoculations for children, food for the starving, and abortions for women impregnated as a result of rape. Ordinary women often took on important roles providing nourishment and clothing, moral and emotional support, and administering first aid to desperate refugees.[59] But professionals and volunteers never met the immense demands.

The refugee crisis of India and Pakistan starting in 1947 set up decades of tensions between the two new nation-states. We can't cover that entire history, but memories of the violence and mass exodus scarred individual and national consciences. The countries later fought four wars and engaged in many more military skirmishes. In India, Hindu nationalism abated after the assassination of Mohandas Gandhi in 1948 by a Hindu nationalist weakened the movement's reputation. Still, the sentiment is on the rise today. Meanwhile, Pakistan emerged as one of the most religiously homogenous nation-states in the world, with over 96 percent of the population practicing Islam (the vast majority of which practices Sunni Islam). However, East Pakistan and West Pakistan found themselves increasingly at odds. By 1971 these conflicts exploded in a horrific genocide of Bangladeshis, igniting a war that resulted in the creation of the nation-state of Bangladesh. Much of the politics of this region of Asia today remains a legacy of the Partition and the refugee crisis it ignited.

Conclusion

The situation in Korea in 1945–1950 bears some remarkable similarities to the cases of Israel/Palestine and India/Pakistan. In the interest of space, I'm going to offer only just enough detail to convince you that all three refugee crises were part of a shared moment in world history associated with decolonization in Asia. From 1392 until the end of the nineteenth century, Korea was ruled by the Chosŏn (also spelled Joseon) dynasty, which had close relations to China. In the nineteenth century, Japanese imperialism transformed the Korean peninsula. In 1876 the Japanese government started practicing "gunboat diplomacy" with Korea, threatening a naval attack unless Korea opened its markets to Japanese traders.[60] Japan further solidified its imperialist reputation with a victory in the Russo-Japanese War (1904–1905), which ensured that Korea fell within Japan's sphere of influence. In 1910, Japan fully annexed Korea.

Under Japanese rule, Korean peasants were forced to produce rice for export to Japan, while the army brutally repressed protestors. At the same time, Koreans gained unprecedented access to global ideas—including nationalism—through

---

59. Virdee, "Negotiating the Past."

60. The United State had successfully used this technique on Japan in 1853–1854.

the same new technologies we have seen elsewhere (steamships, railroads, telegraphs, and newspapers). Though Japan and Korea remained largely unaffected by World War I, Korean anticolonialists also sent representatives to the Paris Peace Conference in 1919 to argue for independence based on the principle of self-determination. Like the Arab, Jewish, and Indian delegates mentioned earlier, the Korean representative came home disappointed.[61]

As elsewhere, this frustration only intensified nationalism. On March 1, 1919 a group of anticolonialists wrote a Korean Declaration of Independence. "We hereby declare," they wrote, "that Korea is an independent state and that Koreans are a self-governing people. We proclaim it to the nations of the world in affirmation of the principle of the equality of all nations."[62] This act sparked the so-called March First Movement, in which over 500,000 Koreans took part in demonstrations for independence. The Japanese government responded by arresting tens of thousands and killing hundreds of protestors.[63] Just as in India and Palestine, in 1919 the Japanese adopted a policy that hung independence out as a future promise without any plan to meet that end. The Japanese called the policy *bunka seiji*, an educational system that promised Koreans a distant but vague future autonomy. Starting in 1927, Japan also encouraged the expansion of a moderate but ineffective nationalist group, Sin'ganhoe, as a way of placating nationalists.[64] After World War II, when the Soviet Union and United States drove Japanese occupiers out of Korea, many nationalists felt that this was the critical moment to establish Korean self-determination. By September 12, 1945, less than a week after Japan's surrender, local citizens in organizations with names like "Committee Preparing for the Restoration of Statehood" proclaimed the Republic of Korea.

Korean nationalists' triumph quickly turned to disorder. The same week that they declared independence, US army officials, fearing that the Soviet Union might take Korea for itself, decided to militarily occupy the southern half of the Korean peninsula. The Republic of Korea established its own government north of that border, which allied with the Soviet Union, and reapportioned land to peasants who had been treated brutally under Japanese rule. For three years, the United States occupied southern Korea, inspiring deep resentments and even a guerrilla insurgency.

As result of these developments, a refugee crisis ignited in Korea. Landowners in North Korea flooded south by the hundreds of thousands. Opponents of the American military occupation moved north (or to China). Today, memory of the

---

61. Manela, *Wilsonian Moment*, 119–35, 197–213.

62. Printed in *Sources of Korean Tradition*, edited by Yŏng-ho Ch'oe, Peter H. Lee, and Wm. Theodore de Bary, vol. 2 (New York: Columbia University Press, 2000), 337–39.

63. Japanese and Korean sources do not agree on the numbers. Bruce Cumings, *Korea's Place in the Sun: A Modern History*, Updated ed. (New York: Norton, 2005), 155.

64. Cumings, *Korea's Place*, 156.

split remains deeply contentious in both North and South Korea. We have better numbers from South Korea than from North, though. Between September 1945 and June 1950, almost two million people fled the north for the south. The military conflict that erupted in June 1950 served as a proxy war between the Soviets and China on one side and the United States on the other. Over half a million people died and entire communities were left devastated. By 1960, over one third of South Korea's population were refugees from the north.[65] The Korean refugee crisis and the war the followed left scars that haunt virtually all politics in Korea today.

Not all decolonization in Asia resulted in a refugee crisis. But colonialism contributed to volatile situations everywhere it was imposed in Asia. As we learned, the very concept of Asia—or the more common term at the time, "Orient"— entailed a European belief that European colonialism in Asia followed the natural order of the world. In 1919, many anticolonialists hoping that this might change actively promoted a relative recent idea—the nation-state—as an alternative. Disappointment in 1919—in all three of our examples—only fueled the spread of nationalism among colonial subjects. By 1945, nationalist dissent proliferated. The logic of the Orient—colonial subjugation—was being replaced by the logic of the nation-state—national self-determination. The history of colonialism in all three places also helps explain why these three refugee crises happened at almost the exact same time. In the last chapter, we'll learn that the guiding principles shaping refugee crises after the decolonization of Africa were a bit different yet.

FURTHER READING

Gilmartin, David. "Partition, Pakistan, and South Asian History," *Journal of Asian Studies* 57, no. 40 (1998): 1068–95.

Khalidi, Rashid. *Palestinian Identity: The Construction of Modern National Consciousness*. New York: Columbia University Press, 2010.

Khan, Yasmin. *The Great Partition: The Making of India and Pakistan*, New ed. New Haven, CT: Yale University Press, 2017.

Manela, Erez. *The Wilsonian Moment: Self-Determination and the International Origins of Anticolonial Nationalism*. Oxford: Oxford University Press, 2007.

Morris, Benny. *The Birth of the Palestinian Refugee Problem Revisited*. Cambridge: Cambridge University Press, 2004.

Talbot, Ian, and Gurharpal Singh. *The Partition of India*. Cambridge: Cambridge University Press, 2009.

Zamindar, Vazira Fazila-Yacoobali. *The Long Partition and the Making of Modern South Asia: Refugees, Boundaries, Histories*. New York: Columbia University Press, 2007.

---

65. Dirk Hoerder, *Cultures in Contact: World Migrations in the Second Millenium* (Durham, NC: Duke University Press, 2002), 486.

5 THE MANY AFRICAS AND REFUGEE CRISES IN ALGERIA, UGANDA, AND THE GREAT LAKES

> Of all the ambiguous words in this universe, the word "African" is surely the top one ... "Who is an African?" At school we were taught that an African was a man who lived in Africa ... Then petty politicians set in ... To them the criterion is rested on the blackness of one's skin and the coarseness of one's hair.[1]

For this anonymous writer in 1964, and for so many more during the era of Africa's decolonization (c. 1950s–1970s), defining "Africa" became central to social and political life. Like other continents, Africa is a geographic space, but also a diverse set of "big ideas." However, many do not comprehend Africa's great diversity. To see what I mean, let's start with a mistake many people make today: talking about "Africa" as if it were a monolithic entity. Try this: type "Africa is not a country" into your favorite internet search engine. I'm confident you'll find that simplistic stereotypes about Africa have proven remarkably resilient. The reality is that the continent is enormously diverse in terms of economics, religion, ecology, politics, genetic variation, and social experience, and these aspects have changed over many

---

1. "Zanzibari," letter to the editor, in *Tanganyika Standard*, April 10, 1964, quoted in Ned Bertz, *Diaspora and Nation in the Indian Ocean: Transnational Histories of Race and Urban Space in Tanzania* (Honolulu: University of Hawai'i Press, 2016), 140.

centuries. Indeed, before European colonialism, the idea of "Africa" did not even exist in most African languages. By the period of decolonization, though—only a few generations later—varied ideas about Africa had become the stuff of mass politics, war, and, of course, refugee crises.

Historians do not know the origins of the term "Africa," but by the second century BC the Roman Empire used "Africa Proconsularis" as the name of a province in present-day northern Africa. When the Muslim Umayyads captured the region in the early eighth century, they called it "Ifriqiya," an Arabic version of the Latin word. During the fifteenth century, as Portuguese explorers traveled Africa's coasts, Europeans first began to use the word to refer to the entire landmass that we think of today, naively lumping diverse peoples together into an undifferentiated group. The first people to call themselves "African" were educated people of African ancestry living in the Americas during the eighteenth century.[2] For them, being "African" connected a collective oppression—slavery—with a mythical sense of a shared homeland. In the nineteenth century, the embrace of African identity grew strong enough in the United States and the Caribbean that it became an intellectual movement: Pan-Africanism.[3] However, the diverse peoples who lived on the African continent still did not see themselves as African.

People living in Africa first embraced African-ness as a consequence of European colonialism. Starting in the 1880s, Europeans divided up the continent through a series of diplomatic agreements, with little consideration for the language or cultures of the people who lived there.[4] This so-called Scramble for Africa formed part of a global transformation that historians call "new imperialism." From the 1880s to the 1910s, the very period when nationalism was intensifying in Western nation-states, leaders of those states also intensified their informal and formal colonial control over most of the world. Preexisting colonial governance—like in India, Algeria, and the American West—intensified. Imperialism expanded into new areas too, including in Africa. New imperialism was partially driven by increasing nationalism, as well as growing global technological and economic divides that emerged as a result of the Second Industrial Revolution. It was also inspired by imperial powers' interest in accessing raw materials, especially rubber and metals required for industrialization. Plus, it provided captive markets for industrially produced goods. That is, new imperialism was both a cause and consequence of industrialization, intensifying nationalism, and a growing global economic divide. In Africa, the arbitrary and violent nature

---

2. Stephanie E. Smallwood, *Saltwater Slavery: A Middle Passage from Africa to American Diaspora* (Cambridge, MA: Harvard University Press, 2007), 187–91.

3. Hakim Adi, *Pan-Africanism: A History* (London: Bloomsbury Academic, 2018).

4. Liberia, founded in 1847 by former slaves from the United States, and the Ethiopian Empire, which repelled an Italian invasion, remained independent from European rule.

Europeans' rule sometimes inspired resistance from locals, which resulted in cata-strophic responses from machine-gun-wielding colonizers.[5]

Indeed, the exploitative and brutal nature of European colonialism first en-couraged some people in Africa to see themselves as having a common cause *as Africans*. We see an early sign of this at a Pan-African Congress in 1919 that met in Paris just as the peace talks ending World War I were underway. The nearly sixty delegates (only some of whom were from Africa) issued a statement calling for self-determination, as well as reparations for slavery and colonialism.[6] In the 1920s and 1930s, African identity spread as opposition to colonialism intensi-fied. But diverse experiences under colonialism meant that the process of what we might call "becoming African" happened differently across the continent. In some cases, this identity bound together people living north and south of the Sahara Desert. Others connected African-ness with an identity as "black."

This chapter looks at how varied colonial histories affected this process of becoming African in ways that help us understand three refugee crises in twentieth-century Africa. We begin with Algeria, where anticolonialists argued that African unity across the continent was necessary to end colonialism. The re-sulting Algerian War (1954–1962) saw massive forced displacements of peoples, first of indigenous Muslim North Africans and then of supporters of French colo-nialism. Our second case study is Uganda under the leadership of Idi Amin (1971–1979), who tapped into deep resentments of nonblacks by expelling Ugandans of South Asian descent. In that case, blackness became central to Amin's claims about African-ness. Our final example explores Hutu–Tutsi conflicts in Africa's Great Lakes Region from the 1950s to the 1990s. There, people distinguished be-tween a supposedly "indigenous" race of African Hutus and "foreign" Tutsis who were supposedly racially akin to Europeans. Over the second half of the century, Hutu–Tutsi conflicts devolved into a self-perpetuating cycle of refugee crises.

Decolonization and the Refugee Crises of the Algerian War

From 1515 to 1830, the Ottoman Empire ruled the lands that today are northern Algeria as a vassal state.[7] While Arabic was the most common language and Sunni Islam the most common religion, there remained considerable diversity, includ-ing a sizeable Jewish community, and significant intermarriage between ethnic

---

5. For an example, see Dominik Schaller, "The Genocide of the Herero and Nama in German South-West Africa, 1904–1907," in *Century of Genocide*, ed. Samuel Totten and William S. Parsons (Hoboken, NJ: Taylor & Francis, 2012), 89–114.

6. Adi, *Pan-Africanism*, 46–48.

7. For an introduction to Algerian history, see Benjamin Stora, *Algeria, 1830–2000: A Short History*, trans. Jane Marie Todd (Ithaca, NY: Cornell University Press, 2001).

groups. In 1830, the French king ordered the invasion of Algeria to revive his bad reputation back home. Though the effort failed—King Charles X's government collapsed that same year—France kept Algeria.[8] In the 1830s and 1840s the government encouraged Europeans to settle in Algeria. The settlers were known variously as *colons* (French for "colonists"), "Europeans," or *pieds noirs* ("black feet," a derogatory reference to their poverty and supposedly uncivilized demeanor). In 1848 a new government incorporated Algeria legally into France. Paradoxically while Algeria was no longer formally a colony, most of its residents were treated as colonized subjects.

The era of "new imperialism" brought an intensification of French control over Algeria. By the 1880s, the French had sent about 350,000 settlers there. By the start of World War I, roughly a million *colons* controlled most of the wealth and valuable land and exploited the locals. From the 1870s, the French government permitted Algeria's Jews citizenship and access to the French-language education necessary for upward social mobility, though they still faced widespread anti-Semitism. As a result, Algeria's Jews occupied an uncomfortable middle position in a brutal colonial system built around a racist social and political hierarchy. Many in the Muslim majority resented that Algeria's Jews stood above them in the pecking order. Yet indigenous Muslims reserved the bulk of their anger for *colons*, who expropriated their land and property and treated them as racial inferiors.

Into the 1940s, anticolonial bitterness galvanized into a powerful opposition movement. By the time that World War II ended, in the spring of 1945, there were widespread calls that all people living in Algeria deserved full citizenship. Resentments deepened because the government diverted food and supplies from destitute people in postwar Algeria to destitute people in postwar France. Thus, on May 8, 1945—Victory in Europe Day—massive demonstrations erupted in Algeria's cities. Protestors carried banners reading "Down with fascism and colonialism," and "Long live a free and independent Algeria."[9] *Colons* had no interest in giving up their privileges, while the indigenous Muslim majority rejected any further exploitation. These resentments simmered to an explosive boil of anticolonial violence in the town of Sétif. Pro-independence protestors attacked police and *colons*, killing around one hundred "Europeans." This violence only reinforced the racism of *colons* and French toward indigenous Muslims. The French army responded by slaughtering thousands of Muslims and bombing forty villages.[10]

8. Jennifer E. Sessions, *By Sword and Plow: France and the Conquest of Algeria* (Ithaca, NY: Cornell University Press, 2011), 264–308.

9. Alistair Horne, *A Savage War of Peace, Algeria 1954–1962* (New York: New York Review Books, 2006), 23–28.

Meanwhile, *colon* vigilantes took Muslim prisoners out of jail to lynch them or simply shot and killed Muslims on the street. Some anticolonial leaders became convinced that violence had become the only way to end colonialism.

Algeria remained polarized and tense into the early 1950s, until anticolonial movements far away inspired an uprising in 1954 that led to a series of refugee crises. In Egypt, a military coup ended British colonialism in 1952. Two years later, in the French colony of Indochina, Ho Chi Minh led a victory against the French army at Dien Bien Phu. Inspired by these anticolonial victories, on October 10, 1954 opposition leaders in Algeria formed the National Liberation Front (*Front de la libération nationale*, or the FLN). On November 1, the FLN's armed wing launched a war for independence. The French government refused to retreat from Algeria, which it regarded as a part of France. There's not space here to cover all the horrors of the Algerian War. Suffice it to say that it was a brutal guerrilla conflict that involved tanks in the streets, widespread torture, massacres, and bombings of civilian populations. Some historians have estimated that roughly 18,000 French soldiers and 10,000 *colons* died, compared to over 1,000,000 Muslim North Africans, though these numbers remain controversial.[11]

During the war, Algeria's anticolonial rebels "became African." FLN leaders came to see African unity as rooted in Africans' common experiences under colonialism, rather than by geography.[12] Africans, according to this view, needed to use violence to repudiate the violence of colonialism, thereby reclaiming African freedom. We can understand how anticolonialism in Algeria drew on Pan-Africanism by turning to the key author who provided an intellectual framework for their resistance. Frantz Fanon, a psychiatrist from Martinique (in the Caribbean), moved to Algeria in 1953, and served as a soldier and later diplomat for the FLN. As he wrote in his 1961 *The Wretched of the Earth* (*Les damnés de la terre*), "The peoples of Africa have only recently come to know themselves. They have decided, in the name of the whole continent, to weigh in strongly against the colonial regime . . . we must understand that African unity can only be achieved through the upward thrust of the people."[13] Fanon argued that colonial

---

10. Estimates of the death toll range from 6,000 to 20,000. Ali Al'Amin Mazrui and Michael Tidy, *Nationalism and New States in Africa from about 1935 to the Present* (Nairobi: Heinemann, 1984), 123. Horne, *A Savage War*, 27.

11. Roland Oliver and Anthony Atmore, *Africa since 1800*, 3rd ed. (Cambridge: Cambridge University Press, 1981), 242.

12. Robert A. Mortimer, "The Algerian Revolution in Search of the African Revolution," *Journal of Modern African Studies* 8, no. 3 (1970): 365–70.

13. Frantz Fanon, *The Wretched of the Earth*, trans. Constance Farrington (New York: Grove Press, 1963), 164.

powers worked to divide Africans—by race, religion, and ethnicity—as a way of enabling their rule. The colonial governments promoted animosities between Africa's Christians and Muslims, he argued, who in fact shared a common cause of unshackling the bonds of colonialism. The same is true of the divide between North African "Arabs" and sub-Saharan "black Africans." Africans must reject such racial differences—which Europeans had constructed in the first place—and embrace African unity. If the French would not leave Algeria voluntarily, Fanon and FLN leaders concluded, a revolution would be required to reclaim Africa for Africans.

The Algerian War spawned massive displacements of peoples. First, the French government forcibly removed peasants from areas it deemed off-limits, mostly in places near Algeria's borders with Morocco and Tunisia where FLN troops were based (see lower left inset of Map 5.1). Following the civilians' removal, the army destroyed their villages so that the FLN could not use them. They moved the displaced people to so-called *regroupement* ("regrouping") camps, allegedly for their own protection.[14] The army prepared a statement for forcibly removed peasants to sign, declaring that "I agree to support the loss of my property as a personal and selfless contribution to . . . the restoration of peace in Algeria."[15] Of course, the document was written in French, so many signers did not understand it. By mid-year 1958, about half a million people—including nomads and semi-nomads—had been "regrouped" into 641 centers. Camp residents faced military supervision and curfews and lived in horrible conditions. None was compensated for their lost property. By 1959, the government implemented its "thousand new villages program," which was a reformed version of the *regroupement* centers. By 1960, the French government had destroyed 8,000 villages and forcibly displaced some 3.5 million individuals.[16] These displaced persons were not refugees according to the definition used in this book—they were forcibly removed as a coercive act of the state. Those moves, however, proved deeply traumatic, and also inspired many refugees to flee Algeria altogether.

---

14. Keith Sutton, "Population Resettlement—Traumatic Upheavals and the Algerian Experience," *Journal of Modern African Studies* 15, no. 2 (1977): 279–300.

15. "*J'accepte de supporter la perte de mon bien à titre contribution personnelle et désintéressée à la lute pour le rétablissement de la paix en Algérie.*" My translation. Quoted from Keith Sutton, "Army Administration Tensions over Algeria's Centres de Regroupement, 1954–1962," *British Journal of Middle Eastern Studies* 26, no. 2 (1999): 248.

16. Amelia H. Lyons, *The Civilizing Mission in the Metropole: Algerian Families and the French Welfare State during Decolonization* (Standford, CA: Stanford University Press, 2013), 157–59.

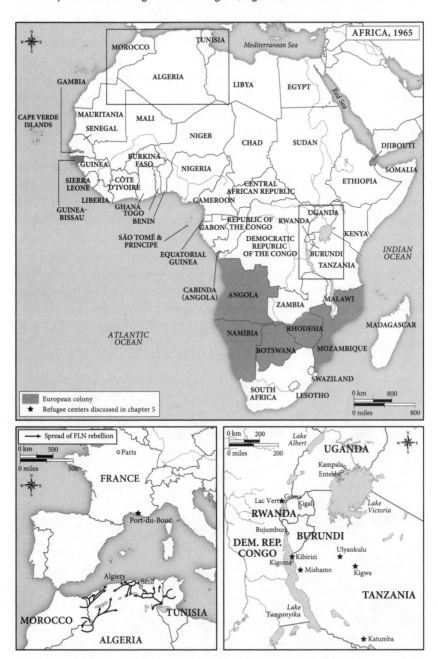

MAP 5.1 Africa, 1965

About 300,000 to 400,000 refugees, almost all women, children, and elderly men, including those photographed in Figure 5.1, fled the violence for neighboring Morocco and Tunisia. They followed the war on Arab-language radio stations using newly available, cheap, battery-operated transistor radios. The two-hour-long daily show "The Voice of Algiers" broadcast a pro-independence message produced by refugees in Cairo. Humanitarian support came from international relief agencies like the Federation of the Red Cross and Red Crescent Societies, Red Barna (Save the Children, Norway), and Quaker organizations like the American Friends Service Committee and Britain's Oxfam. From September 1958, a rebel government in exile had formed, based in Tunisia. One of its members, Frantz Fanon, edited a journal that presented his Pan-African vision. Soon after, he promoted his Pan-Africanism as a diplomat in Ghana, which had gained independence from Britain in 1957. By March 1962, the brutal war in Algeria finally ended with a cease-fire. According to the Evian Peace Accords, Algeria held a referendum to determine whether it should break from France. Ninety-eight percent of voters supported independence. The government in exile returned and began setting up a new state. Independent Algeria's first president, Ahmed Ben Bella, promoted the idea that Africa was defined not by race or geography, but by the shared struggle against colonialism.

FIGURE 5.1 Nearly 200,000 refugees crossed into Tunisia and Morocco by 1960, most of whom were women, children, and the elderly.
Source: UNHCR

The war's aftermath produced refugee crises as well. Questions lingered about what would happen to the nearly one million "European" *colons*, but also 120,000 Algerian Jews, and over 250,000 indigenous soldiers who had fought for the French. Algeria's new leaders argued for the immediate departure of all three groups. One proposed solution was for *pieds noirs* to migrate to Latin America. Plans developed to create a settlement in Paraguay.[17] By April 1961, French President Charles de Gaulle's government reluctantly decided that France had to accept *pieds noirs* and Algerian Jews. But only a few started moving. The trickle of migration turned into a flood of refugees after June 17, when the pro-French paramilitary group—called the Secret Army Organization (*Organisation de l'armée secrète*, or OAS)—conceded to the FLN. Without OAS protection, the *pieds noirs* faced brutal retaliation if they stayed. Thousands of refugees descended on Algeria's ports, looking for ships bound for France. Entire families travelled together, often under the flimsy pretense that they were taking a summer vacation. Colonists sold their cars for a pittance or just abandoned them. Shopkeepers liquidated their stocks. "Let's face it" one French official explained, "the whole of Algeria is up for sale."[18] During the summer of 1962, some 750,000 *pieds noirs* fled Algeria. By December 1963, that number had risen to roughly 900,000.

The French government requisitioned all kinds of buildings as temporary shelters to house the refugees—including castles, schools, convents, hospitals, factories, and barracks. In 1963 officials planned the construction of 35,000 low-income apartments for *pieds noirs*, as well as 10,000 houses. But these efforts were paltry compared to the overwhelming need. The mayor of one town, Port-du-Bouc, explained that multiple families shared one-bedroom apartments, while two- and three-bedroom apartments housed up to twenty individuals. Some people, he explained, were building their own shantytowns.[19]

Nearly the entire Algerian Jewish population fled with the *pieds noirs* to France.[20] In their own writings, they drew parallels between their escape from Algeria and the ancient Israelites' exodus from Egypt. Many of the Jewish refugees arrived without any proof of French citizenship or knowledge of French. The United Jewish Social Fund (*Fonds social juif unifié*) struggled to provide them housing, food, schooling, and employment and to build new synagogues.

---

17. In February 1962 some resettled to Brazil, through the program was abandoned because it was costly and difficult. Sung-Eun Choi, *Decolonization and the French of Algeria: Bringing the Settler Colony Home* (London: Palgrave Macmillan, 2016), 55.

18. Quoted in Horne, *A Savage War*, 532.

19. Choi, *Decolonization*, 60.

20. Todd Shepard, *The Invention of Decolonization: The Algerian War and the Remaking of France* (Ithaca, NY: Cornell University Press, 2006), 169–82. The state of Israel offered welcome to Algeria's Jewish refugees, though few took this option.

Curiously, the French government designated Algerian Jewish refugees—as it did for *pied noir* refugees—as "repatriates," as if they were merely reuniting with their country. After all, since the French government had long considered Algeria a part of France, than legally speaking, they had previously lived in France. Now that Algeria was no longer part France, they had move to the European continent to be "repatriated." But this was little more than a legal fiction. For all practical purposes, they were not being repatriated but escaping to a new land that was unfamiliar to them.

Many harkis—indigenous Muslim soldiers who had fought for France—sought to flee as well.[21] A United Nations report written in the spring of 1962 estimated that there were about 263,000 of them, and FLN soldiers were hunting them down as collaborators and traitors. Frightened harkis petitioned for protection in France. As one wrote on May 1962: "I categorically refuse to stay in an Algerian Algeria ... I am French and want to remain in France with my family."[22] But the idea of welcoming Muslims met with resistance from the French population. On May 23, 1962 President Charles de Gaulle explained that harki refugees would become a drain on local charities. Their young women would turn to prostitution, he warned, implying that harkis posed a threat to monogamy in France.[23] De Gaulle proposed relocating the harkis to a desolate region in Chad, which had gained independence peacefully in 1960, though Chadian President François Tombalbaye quickly rejected the idea. To receive permission to enter France, a harki needed to provide documentation of an individual and immediate threat, rather than the general danger facing all harkis. Such requirements made legal migration practically impossible, despite the fact that most were French citizens. Meanwhile, a humanitarian disaster was unfolding; some estimates have suggested that as many as 100,000 harkis were killed in Algeria after the war.[24] By the end of 1962, roughly half of the harki families had made it to France, sometimes with assistance from French soldiers who had fought alongside them. The government sent most to former prison camps, renamed Welcome Cities (*Cités d'Accueil*), where the harkis lived under military surveillance far from large populations of local French people. Refugees lived in simple shelters and worked at nearby locations, mostly in forestry.[25]

---

21. The term "harki" comes from the Arabic term for movement (*haraka*). It originally referred to a section of Muslim infantry, but gradually came to be used for any Muslim serving in the French army in Algeria.

22. Quoted in Shepard, *Invention of Decolonization*, 235.

23. Shepard, *Invention of Decolonization*, 230–33.

24. Stora, *Algeria*, 101.

25. Choi, *Decolonization*, 70–71.

Back in Algeria, millions of people exiled during the war, forced into *re-groupement* camps, or otherwise displaced, started returning.[26] The United Nations High Commissioner for Refugees (UNHCR), which in 1950 had replaced the International Refugee Organization, began assisting many of the roughly 300,000 refugees who had lived abroad, supported by the League of the Red Cross and Red Crescent Societies. In all, about two thirds of those who had lived in Tunisia and Morocco returned to Algeria, while the rest integrated into their host societies. Meanwhile, some peasants who had been forced into the *regroupement* camps just stayed there, since the French army had destroyed their villages. Most of the rest moved into Algeria's cities, often taking over abandoned apartments left by the *pieds noirs*. As a result, Algeria emerged as a more urbanized and less nomadic and pastoral country that it had been previously.

During the war, Algeria became a powerful symbol for Pan-Africanism. The message of Frantz Fanon and other FLN leaders expressed a shared struggle against colonialism that tied together peoples across Africa, and around the world.[27] As the FLN's ambassador in Ghana, Fanon also interacted with Kwame Nkrumah, probably the most influential African leader of the 1950s and 1960s, and another consummate Pan-Africanist. While historians have rightly contrasted Fanon's belief that decolonization demanded violence and Nkrumah's commitment to nonviolence, the two men shared a belief that supposed racial divisions between "blacks" and "Arabs" threatened African unity. As Fanon asserted to Nkrumah and others in Ghana in December 1958: "Africa is at war with colonialism." Earlier that same year, Nkrumah wrote: "From Algeria in the North to Nigeria in the West, from Kenya in the East to the tribes in the South, Africans bemoan their fate against the atrocities of colonialism!" for the "whole of Africa trembles under the impact of colonial brutalities."[28] As we'll see, other colonial legacies led to deep divisions *between* colonial subjects in Africa that contrasted with Nkrumah and Fanon's dream, and led to dramatically different outcomes.

---

26. Ammar Bouhouche, "The Return of Algerian Refugees following Independence in 1962," in *When Refugees Go Home: African Experiences*, ed. Tim Allen and Hubert Morsink (Trenton, NJ: Africa World Press, 1994), 74–76.

27. For Algeria's role in the so-called Third World Movement, see Robert Malley, *The Call from Algeria: Third Worldism, Revolution, and the Turn to Islam* (Berkeley: University of California Press, 1996).

28. Both quotes come from Jeffrey S. Ahlman, "The Algerian Question in Nkrumah's Ghana, 1958–1960: Debating 'Violence' and 'Nonviolence' in African Decolonization," *Africa Today* 57, no. 2 (2010): 71, 74.

Decolonization, Africanization, and the Expulsion of Uganda's Asians

Uganda gained its independence in 1962, the same year as Algeria, but the refugee crisis that it experienced was shaped by a different colonial history, which reflected East Africa's long relationship to the Indian Ocean world. Arab and Indian traders had involved themselves in the region for centuries. After the Scramble for Africa, Hindus and Muslims from British India also moved there, initially recruited by the British as soldiers and railroad workers.[29] In Uganda, a simplistic three-part racial division came to define most social relations. At the top of the hierarchy were Europeans. Though small in number, they occupied positions of authority in government and business. They mostly spoke English and received education in European schools. At the bottom were black Africans, whom most people simply called "Africans." Most received no formal education, were banned from owning businesses, and spoke their native language (of which there were many), along with Swahili, the trade language of East Africa. The British government exploited black Africans for their labor, but it also defined them by ethnicity, rather than race. This served British interests in promoting divisions among black Africans, and treating their cultures as fixed (and therefore not capable of Western "progress"). In the middle of this hierarchy were the so-called Asians, a racial category describing people of Indian extraction. Unlike black Africans, thus, legally defining Asians as a race both ignored the ethnic differences among Asians, and defined them as "biologically" foreign to Africa. The British invested in a separate educational system for these people, who learned English, Gujarati, and Urdu. Their English-language education meant that they could serve as lower colonial administrators. Uganda's Asians were also restricted from land ownership, which pushed them into work as traders and businesspeople. By 1914, Asians controlled as much as 90 percent of Uganda's trade. Over time, living in this racialized legal and political system deeply affected all the individuals within it. Europeans often deepened their sense of self-confidence and white supremacy. Somewhat like Algeria's Jews, Uganda's Asians held a kind of a middle position between the European colonists at the top, and the majority of the colonized subjects. For the most part, they remained culturally isolated. Uganda's black Africans came to resent the Asians, because they held roles that supported the colonial government and economy that they despised. In that way, the anger Uganda's Asians faced from Uganda's black Africans was also a bit like the resentment faced by Algeria's Jews from indigenous Muslims, in that the colonial system established them both as racialized foreigners with greater privileges than the marginalized majority.

---

29. J. S. Mangat, *A History of the Asians in East Africa*, 1896–1945 (Oxford: Clarendon Press, 1969), 27–46.

As in Algeria, Pan-African independence movements in Uganda started in the 1920s, but did not gain widespread traction until after World War II. In 1945, a general strike against British colonialism provided the same kind of spark of mass anticolonialism that we saw with the Sétif massacre in Algeria. In 1952, the Uganda National Congress (UNC) formed on the model of the Indian National Congress. Anticolonialists called for *uhuru*, a Swahili word for freedom analogous to the Hindi word *swaraj*, discussed in chapter 4.[30] That is, anticolonialists used an indigenous *African* idea to argue for self-determination, rather than looking only to Western systems of thought.

After independence, a central challenge in promoting uhuru was the fact that Uganda's political leaders inherited the same weak bureaucracies, economic inequalities, and ethnic divisions promoted under British colonial rule. In this situation, the military proved to be the most robust national institution, as well as the most reliable instrument for protecting the administration. Thus in February 1966, when President Milton Obote's coalition faced a challenge from the Baganda people in the south, he sent troops to repress dissent.[31] After this, Obote increasingly emerged as a repressive dictator. But Obote's greatest strength—the military—was also his greatest vulnerability. In January 1971 Idi Amin, the same general who helped him orchestrate the 1966 campaign, deposed Obote.

Ugandans warmly embraced Amin at first, though the honeymoon proved short-lived. The general promised adoring crowds democracy, security, the rule of law, reduced taxes, and economic development.[32] He also reconciled with the Baganda, released political prisoners, and began building positive relations with Britain, the Arab world, and Israel.[33] Amin presented himself also a hypermasculine figure who exuded confidence and power (though he was barely literate): he had been a heavyweight boxing champion, had served in the famed King's African Rifles, and had risen to the highest rank possible for a black African in the British colonial army. But Amin could never deliver on his promises. For starters, Obote still had supporters in the army. In addition, Amin's promises were farcically unrealistic. Like his predecessor, the army proved to be Amin's most reliable tool for responding to challenges that arose. By July 1972 a failed coup convinced him to

30. Tom Mboya, *The Mass Movement* (1963), printed in Elie Kedourie, ed. *Nationalism in Asia and Africa* (London: Frank Cass, 1970), 478, 86.

31. Phares Mutibwa, *Uganda since Independence: A Story of Unfulfilled Hopes* (Trenton, NJ: Africa World Press, 1992), 37–41.

32. Mahmood Mamdani, *Imperialism and Fascism in Uganda* (Trenton, NJ: Africa World Press, 1984), 37–38.

33. Mazrui and Tidy, *Nationalism*, 250–51. Mutibwa, *Uganda*, 78–87. There are suspicions that Britain and Israel backed Amin's coup, because Obote had criticized Britain's sale of arms to the apartheid government in South Africa.

begin a violent purge of the military. Amin responded to civilian protests with harsh repression as well.

A year and a half into his reign, on August 4, 1972, Amin announced that Uganda's seventy thousand Asians had to leave the country within ninety days. From one perspective, this action might have been surprising. Initially most Asians supported independence in 1962. The Uganda Action Group, a political associa- tion founded by Asians, declared support for Milton Obote's new government.[34] Some Asians had also supported Amin's coup in 1972.

We might understand Amin's decision as a particularly cruel and vindictive ver- sion of a larger process called "Africanization." In decolonizing regions of sub-Saha- ran Africa, this term described the process of establishing black African control over the institutions of political and economic power. In other forms, Africanization could express a powerful and positive message: Africans deserved to have access to the resources and knowledge previously barred them, to promote self-rule and self- actualization. The targets of Africanization were usually people of European heri- tage who had inherited wealth and privilege in the colonies. In Uganda, however, the British had created a situation in which peoples of Indian descent had acquired resources and knowledge not allowed to most black Africans. Many black Africans thus blamed Uganda's Asians for complicity in British colonialism. Resentments were real and ran deep. Under Idi Amin's dictatorship, Asians became targets of Africanization though expulsion as well. As a result, unlike in Algeria, embracing African identity in Uganda became deeply connected with blackness.

Idi Amin's expulsion of Asians also provided the dictator with a useful scapegoat capable of diverting attention from his own failures. Soon into his rule, Uganda's economy began faltering, prices climbed, taxes had not fallen, and violent crime was getting worse. Targeting Asians helped Amin promote solidar- ity among black Africans, lest rivalries between different ethnicities destabilize his rule. From his first days as a public figure, Amin complained about Asians' failure to assimilate, questioned their loyalty, and accused them of supporting co- lonialism. By the end of 1971, Amin blamed the country's financial downfall on Asians, who he argued were hoarding goods to create shortages, and committing financial fraud aimed at enriching themselves and impoverishing black Africans. As Amin told his former commanding officer, Iain Graham, Uganda's Asians "have cheated the black people in this country for too long. Uganda wants full economic independence and [black Africans] can only get this when [Uganda's Asians] go."[35] Expelling Asians also provided an influx of seized wealth into state coffers. The expulsion proved enormously popular among Ugandans.[36] Groups

---

34. Mangat, *History of the Asians*, 176–77.

35. Iain Grahame, *Amin and Uganda: A Personal Memoir* (London: Granada, 1980), 133.

such as the Uganda African Traders' Association and students at Makerere University supported the act. Uganda's Defense Council awarded Amin eight honors and metals to celebrate the expulsion. Not a single newspaper or major press outlet criticized the order—and many celebrated it. Amin's decision had the overwhelming support of the country's black African population.

Between September and November of 1972 some 50,000 Asian refugees fled Uganda. Basically an entire class of traders who had managed much of the country's industrial and commercial system disappeared. Most left with little more than the clothes on their back, while the government appropriated their homes and property. Soldiers also seized jewelry, watches, and luggage as refugees made their way to the airport at Entebbe. The majority—some 30,000—sought asylum in Britain, while others went to India, Pakistan, Bangladesh, Canada, and the United States. Refugees, like those disembarking an airplane in a foreign land in Figure 5.2, left behind property and businesses worth some £500 million.[37]

FIGURE 5.2 Unlike previous examples, the Uganda Asian refugee crises took place on airplanes.
Source: PA Archive/PA Images

36. Mamdani, *Imperialism and Fascism*, 40.

37. Mazrui and Tidy, *Nationalism*, 280.

Uganda's government quickly established committees whose job it was to distribute all the "abandoned" property. A team of military officers—including Amin's notorious hitman, Isaac Maliyamungu—helped the committees distribute property to loyalists, including themselves. This massive redistribution of wealth created a new social class as fast as it eliminated the previous one. The so-called *mafuta mingi* (a Swahili term meaning "too much fat" used to describe the wealthy) enjoyed the spoils of the expulsion, which gave them unsurpassed political and economic dominance. Because of the loss in knowledge of trade and finance it entailed, Amin's expulsion of Uganda's Asians helped contribute to the further devastation of Uganda's economy in the 1970s.[38] The Uganda case demonstrates how resentments that resulted from colonial policies could lead to vastly different understandings of African unity. In this case, Africanization encouraged a hostility of black Africans toward those nonblack colonial subjects who had been privileged under colonialism.

In Britain, the relocation of Uganda's Asian refugees was coordinated by the Uganda Resettlement Board, which identified temporary residences for some five thousand Ugandan refugees in private homes and established sixteen camps for the rest.[39] Refugees had to learn the basics of life in an industrialized society, including how to use Western-style toilets. Back in Uganda, Asian women did not take employment outside the house. In Britain, many were forced to enter the labor market.[40] In London, protestors marched with signs displaying messages like "Britain for the British" or "No More Asians." Rumors circulated that the Ugandan Asians promoted crime and illegal drugs. Graffiti displayed racist anti-immigrant language. Some refugees faced physical abuse. Many Britons slowly warmed to the idea of welcoming the refugees, however, after news of Amin's cruelties became widely reported in the international press.[41]

The experience of moving from Uganda to Britain taught these families an important lesson about racial differences, which we can learn about through one refugee memoir.[42] Mahmood Mamdani, who was twenty-six when he fled

---

38. Mutibwa, *Uganda*, 115–24.

39. Jordanna Bailkin, *Unsettled: Refugee Camps and the Making of Multicultural Britain* (Oxford: Oxford University Press, 2018), 55–64. William G. Kuepper, G. Lynne Lackey, and E. Nelson Swinerton, *Ugandan Asians in Great Britain: Forced Migration and Social Absorption* (New York: New Viewpoints, 1975), 62–68.

40. Joanna Herbert, "Oral Histories of Ugandan Asians in Britain: Gendered Identities in the Diaspora," *Contemporary South Asia* 17, no. 1 (2009): 21–32.

41. Becky Taylor, "Good Citizens? Ugandan Asians, Volunteers, and 'Race' Relations in 1970s Britain," *History Workshop Journal* 85, no. 1 (2018): 120–41.

42. Mahmood Mamdani, *From Citizen to Refugee: Uganda Asians Come to Britain*, 2nd ed. (Cape Town: Pambazuka Press, 2011), 69, 86–87.

Uganda, recalled being visited in the camps by people of Indian descent who had been born in Britain, who explained "we blacks must unite and defend ourselves . . . and fight for Black Power." Why were they so confused? Mamdani was quite clear *he* was not black. Later, Mamdani told the story of a group of white Britons who yelled at a Ugandan Asian, "Hey blackie, what are you doing here? Why don't you go home?" A group of black people from the West Indies—perhaps immigrants from Jamaica—stepped in to defend the Ugandan Asians. After the taunters ran away, one of the West Indian men explained, "Look here, brother, it may have been different in Africa. But here, we are all brothers. For the white man, we are [all] black." Mamdani had only fled Uganda because it seemed obvious to everyone in that context that he was not black. But in Britain, the white majority often lumped nonwhites together. As result, rather than people of Indian and black African descent becoming adversaries, they became allies. The refugees learned in a deeply personal way that racial categories were not based in biology, but were the outcome of different historical experiences of inequality.

Racialized Politics and Refugee Crises around Africa's Great Lakes

Our last case study of refugee crises in postcolonial Africa is that of Hutu and Tutsi refugees in Africa's Great Lakes Region, encompassing Rwanda, Burundi, southern Uganda, eastern Democratic Republic of the Congo, and northwestern Tanzania (see lower right inset of Map 5.1). Before getting into the details, it's important to understand that Hutus and Tutsis were not separate "tribes" that had some primordial conflict going back centuries. In fact, the notion of "tribes" in Africa can be problematic, because European colonists often invented tribal categories to organize their rule. Archaeologists like Scott MacEachern can help us differentiate between genetics and malleable terms like "tribe."[43] Neither are Hutus and Tutsis distinct ethnicities, since they speak the same language— Kinyarwanda—and share the same general belief systems. In its origins, the distinction between Hutu and Tutsi is one of a social or political identity.[44] Before the Scramble for Africa, the Kingdoms of Rwanda and Burundi had come to be dominated by a minority population called Tutsis, who distinguished themselves from Hutus, who made up 85 percent of the population. Some Hutus gained

---

43. Scott MacEachern, "Genes, Tribes, and African History," *Current Anthropology* 41, no. 3 (2000): 357–84.

44. Mahmood Mamdani, *When Victims Become Killers: Colonialism, Nativism, and the Genocide in Rwanda* (Princeton, NJ: Princeton University Press, 2001), 41–75. Gérard Prunier, *The Rwanda Crisis* (New York: Columbia University Press, 1995), 5–40.

access to privilege and power and members of the two groups did intermarry and interact, but both kingdoms were generally organized around this social/political hierarchy. By the end of World War I, Belgium had become a dominant colonial power in the region, including in the Congo (from 1908) and a combined territory called Ruanda-Urundi (from 1916). In the Congo, the Belgian government categorized subjects by ethnic group. Thus it treated all Kinyarwanda-speakers in the eastern Congo the same, and distinguished them from other ethnic groups. As in British Uganda, this practice helped Belgian administrators promote divisions between indigenous populations, making them easier to rule. In contrast, for Ruanda-Urundi the Belgians used the Hutu–Tutsi divide as the organizing feature of life, which as we'll see had a dramatically different outcome.[45]

The Belgians explained why the Tutsis were politically dominant using a theory that the Tutsi "race" was biologically superior to Hutus. This theory of racial superiority matched European worldviews that were developing in the nineteenth century—which we learned about in chapter 3—that explained Western global dominance as a natural expression of white supremacy. However, applying this racist ideology to Ruanda-Urundi required a bit of intellectual gymnastics. Tutsis, Europeans assumed, were superior to Hutus because they were not really "African," but descended from Semitic peoples—the ancestors of Japheth, Shem, and Ham described in chapter 1. The descendants of Ham, remember, were supposed to have gone to Africa. According to this theory, the so-called Hamites brought Caucasian "progress" to the inferior races of sub-Saharan Africa. In 1934, the German linguist Diedrich Westermann explained how the "Hamite" Tutsis differed in appearance from the "Negroid" Hutus:

> They [Hamites] are light skinned, with a straight nose, thin lips, narrow face, soft, often wavy or even straight hair, without prognathism [a protruding jaw] . . . Owing to their racial superiority they have gained leading positions and have become the founders of many of the larger states of Africa.[46]

Westermann claimed that simply looking like a European explained political dominance. Tutsis' supposedly slender noses, for instance, provided an outward demonstration of their inward mental and biological superiority. He also asserted clear physical distinctions between Hutus and Tutsis that simply did not exist.

Scholars do not all agree about who was most responsible for entrenching the Hutu–Tutsi racial divide in Ruanda-Urundi. The political scientist René Lemarchand

---

45. A third Kinyarwanda-speaking group, the Twa, made up only 1 percent of the population of Ruanda-Urundi.

46. Diedrich Westermann, *The African To-Day* (London: Humphrey Milford, 1934), 23–24. See also Peter Kallaway, "Diedrich Westermann and the Ambiguities of Colonial Science in the Inter-War Era," *Journal of Imperial & Commonwealth History* 45, no. 6 (2017): 871–93.

argues that the Belgian government hardened a more fluid precolonial distinction in order to make its colony more governable.[47] The professor of government (and former refugee from Uganda discussed earlier) Mahmood Mamdani agrees, and assigns particular importance to Catholic missionaries in promoting the Hamitic racial theory.[48] The church historian Jay Carney argues that early twentieth-century Catholic missionaries had more flexible and nuanced understandings of race than Mamdani suggests.[49] Still, there is no disagreement that the Hamitic theory legitimized the Belgian government's systematic privileging of Tutsis over Hutus. Subjects received ID cards indicating whether they were Hutu or Tutsi. All aspects of colonial administration, including taxes, schooling, and employment were organized around this hierarchy. As foreign non-African "Hamites," Tutsis learned about their supposed racial superiority in Belgian-run schools, where they also learned French (in addition to Kinyarwanda and Swahili) to prepare them to serve as low-ranking bureaucrats. Meanwhile, the Belgians assigned most Hutus roles as peasants and forced them to grow cash crops like coffee and cotton for export. In a way, European colonialists placed Tutsis in the kind of racialized middle group that Algeria's Jews and Uganda's Asians found themselves in, which was legally, socially, and politically inferior to their European overlords, but superior to the majority population. And like with Uganda's Asians, because the colonial government recruited this racialized group to serve in political and economically privileged positions, in Ruanda-Urundi Hutus deeply resented Tutsis' "foreign" oppression. In both colonies the majority of Africans viewed a racialized minority (Asians or Tutsis) as foreigners guilty of collaboration with European colonial rulers. Meanwhile, across the border in the Congo the Belgian government treated Hutus and Tutsis as part of the same ethnicity, so tensions between these two groups did not develop.

By 1960, as decolonization was sweeping Africa, the Belgian government abruptly pulled out of its African colonies. In the Congo, the Pan-Africanist Patrice Lumumba won the first presidential election that May. Within months, however, Belgium and the United States helped an army leader, Joseph-Désiré Mobutu, topple Lumumba's government.[50] The new dictator renamed himself Mobutu Sese Seko and renamed the country Zaire. Meanwhile, a plan to keep Rwanda and Burundi united after independence failed in the face of

---

47. René Lemarchand, *The Dynamics of Violence in Central Africa* (Philadelphia: University of Pennsylvania Press, 2009), 7–10.

48. Mamdani, *When Victims Become Killers*, 76–102.

49. J. J. Carney, "Beyond Tribalism: The Hutu-Tutsi Question and Catholic Rhetoric in Colonial Rwanda," *Journal of Religion in Africa* 42, no. 2 (2012): 172–202.

50. The United States intervened because Lumumba had reached out to the Soviet Union. The Belgian government worried that Africanization would threaten its financial interests in the Congo. Guy Arnold, *Africa: A Modern History, 1945–2015* (London: Atlantic Books, 2005), 21–27, 77–83.

Hutu–Tutsi tensions. The Belgians helped establish a Tutsi-dominated monarchy in Burundi—replicating colonial hierarchies in the new state. In Rwanda, Hutu intellectuals in 1957 had produced the so-called Bahutu Manifesto, which called for self-determination and an end to both white *and* "Hamite" Tutsi colonialism. In 1959, Belgian leaders supported Hutu nationalists when they launched a revolution.[51] The revolutionaries killed some twenty Tutsi chiefs and over 350 subchiefs and forced many Tutsi leaders to flee Rwanda. A Tutsi counterattack was brutally repressed. Hutus called Tutsis "cockroaches" (*inyenzi*), using the same kind of dehumanizing rhetoric that we have seen in other episodes of mass violence. By mid-1960, more than 130,000 Tutsis had fled Rwanda to neighboring Uganda, Tanzania, Burundi, and Zaire. The new Rwandan state promoted Hutu supremacy and made little effort to integrate the Tutsi minority into the national community. In schools, students learned of the colonial domination of the Hamitic Tutsis and the heroic achievements of the 1959–1962 revolution. Meanwhile, the so-called fifty-niners, Tutsi refugees who had fled Rwanda during the revolution, retained bitter memories of losing their social and political dominance, to say nothing of their homes and loved ones. A failed attack from fifty-niners in 1963 inspired repression that only deepened the divide.

Back in Burundi, Hutus dreamed of a revolution like the one in Rwanda. Failed coups in 1965, 1968, and 1969, however, were met with brutal government retaliation, which only increased polarization. The most impactful effort came in the spring of 1972, when Hutu rebels launched another attempted coup. The Burundian government, led by the dictator Michel Micombero, responded with a genocidal campaign of repression from May to August unlike any of the violence thus far.[52] That summer, Burundi's army massacred somewhere between 80,000 and 250,000 Hutu civilians, whom they called "pythons."[53] This genocide only confirmed for Hutus what they already believed: that Tutsis aimed to exterminate Hutus from the face of the earth. Hundreds of thousands of Hutus left Burundi for Rwanda, Tanzania, and Zaire.

Resentments simmered among many of Burundi's Hutu refugees. The anthropologist Liisa Malkki studied such views in refugee communities that developed in Tanzania following the 1972 genocide.[54] The United Nations High Commissioner for Refugees (UNHCR), the Tanzanian government, and the

---

51. Prunier, *The Rwanda Crisis*, 41–54.

52. René Lemarchand, *Burundi: Ethnic Conflict and Genocide* (Cambridge: Cambridge University Press, 1994), 76–105.

53. For different death counts, Lemarchand, *Burundi*, 100. Liisa H. Malkki, *Purity and Exile: Violence, Memory, and National Cosmology among Hutu Refugees in Tanzania* (Chicago: University of Chicago Press, 1995), 32–33.

54. Malkki, *Purity and Exile*.

Tanganyika Christian Refugee Service funded refugee camps at Kibirizi, which provided escapees with medical care, education, and housing. Later, refugee settlements were built at Ulyankulu, Katumba, Mishamo, and Kigwa, where refugees retold stories of Hutu victimhood and Tutsi wickedness. Many saw their tribulations mirrored in the sufferings of ancient Israelites recounted in the Christian Bible. The refugees also believed that they embodied the Hutu nation, whose lands were occupied by "foreign" Tutsi invaders. In their mythic history, the Belgians had even come to Burundi to protect the peaceful Hutus from "Hamite" tyranny. A militant movement known as Hutu Power flourished in the camps. By the late 1980s, children of exiles who had never met a Tutsi or visited Burundi still believed that Tutsis had a genocidal hunger to kill them.[55]

Not all Hutu refugees fleeing the Burundi genocide developed such embittered views. Those who moved to Tanzanian cities, such as Kigoma, integrated into the local population, taking jobs and intermarrying with locals.[56] Rather than building an identity around Hutu victimhood, they shed their Hutu-ness and adopted Tanzanian identities. Of course, since these refugees did not leave records of themselves *as refugees,* it is difficult for historians to record their influence. The case of Kigoma is a useful reminder that victimhood does not always produce cycles of violence; how one experiences life after suffering plays a large role in how humans respond to tragedy.

Meanwhile, leading Tutsi refugees living in Uganda—including prominent fifty-niners—plotted Rwanda's "liberation" from Hutus. By 1987 this group took a militaristic approach, branding itself the Rwandan Patriotic Front (*Front patriotique rwandais,* known in English as the RPF). In October 1990, the RPF invaded Rwanda, under the leadership of Paul Kagame, with assistance from Uganda and the United States.[57] RPF leadership believed that Rwanda's government would collapse because of its economic problems, military weakness, and a lack of popular support for President Juvénal Habyarimana. But the invaders sorely underestimated anti-Tutsi sentiments among Rwanda's Hutu majority, who rallied around Habyarimana's warnings that the RPF intended to reinstall the pre-1959 Tutsi "tyranny."[58] They also failed to anticipate that Habyarimana would get military support from France, which had economic interests in the country.

In the civil war that followed, the RPF used mass forced displacement as a weapon. In November 1992, the British journalist Catherine Watson reported

55. Marc Sommers, *Fear in Bongoland: Burundi Refugees in Urban Tanzania* (New York: Berghahn Books, 2001).

56. Malkki, *Purity and Exile*, 153–96.

57. Prunier, *The Rwanda Crisis*, 93–126.

58. Lemarchand, *Dynamics of Violence*, 81.

that 10 percent of the entire population of Rwanda—amounting to more than 700,000 mostly Hutus—had been displaced by RPF attacks.[59] By February 1994, that number had risen to 930,000 people, a third of whom had been displaced two, three, and four times as rebels advanced. Meanwhile, Habyarimana grew closer to factions associated with Hutu Power. Some Hutus argued that the only way to save themselves from genocide was to eradicate Tutsis. The first to argue this view publicly was Léon Mugesera, who allegedly told a crowd in 1992 that "We the [Hutu] people are obliged to take responsibility ourselves and wipe out this [Tutsi] scum."[60]

By August 1993, the RPF had made enough gains to force Habyarimana to agree to a power-sharing arrangement. Many Hutus saw compromise as unacceptable. Hutu Power propaganda poured out of pro-Hutu newspapers and radio stations, especially the Thousand Hills Free Radio and Television (*Radio Télévision Libre de Mille Collines*). The newspaper *Kangura* also printed militant anti-Tutsi messages, recalling Tutsi domination before 1959, the genocide in Burundi in 1972, and the current RPF atrocities as evidence that Tutsis were inherently evil people who sought to annihilate Hutus. *Kangura* also warned readers about the treachery of Tutsi women, who supposedly used their beauty to lure disloyal Hutu men. Propagandists called such men traitors to the Hutu race.[61]

Events unfolding in neighboring Burundi worsened the already-dire situation in Rwanda. In the late 1980s, Hutu resistance to Tutsi minority rule escalated. In 1988, violent confrontations resulted in the massacre of as many as 150,000 Hutus, and the flight into foreign lands of tens of thousands more.[62] In response, the government instituted reforms that led to the country's first multiparty elections. On June 1, 1993, 66 percent of the voters chose Melchior Ndadaye—a moderate Hutu politician and intellectual—as the next president.[63] Not even five months later, members of the Tutsi-dominated army assassinated Ndadaye. News of the president's death sparked outrage. In two months, Hutu militants killed an estimated 20,000 Tutsis. The Tutsi-led army responded by killing roughly equal numbers of Hutus and caused what the UNHCR estimated as 500,000 Hutus to flee Burundi. About 340,000 escaped north to Rwanda, while others went to eastern Zaire and Tanzania.[64]

---

59. Catherine Watson, "War and Waiting," *Africa Report*, November/December 1992, 55.

60. Quoted in Mamdani, *When Victims Become Killers*, 195.

61. Lemarchand, *Dynamics of Violence*, 60–63.

62. Lemarchand, *Burundi*, 118–30.

63. Matthias Basedau, "Burundi," in *Elections in Africa: A Data Handbook*, ed. Dieter Nohlen, Michael Krennerich, and Berhard Thibaut (Oxford: Oxford University Press, 1999), 162.

64. Experts disagree about these numbers. Arnold, *Africa*, 857. Lemarchand, *Dynamics of Violence*, 84. Mamdani, *When Victims Become Killers*, 204–05. Malkki, *Purity and Exile*, 261.

Back in Rwanda, the response to Ndadaye's assassination was widespread kill-ings and looting targeting Tutsis. Further, on April 6, 1994, someone launched a missile at a plane carrying the presidents of both Burundi and Rwanda, killing both men.[65] Within forty-five minutes of the attack, a pro-Hutu militia called Interahamwe had blockaded roads out of the country. Radio hosts on Thousand Hills Free Radio and Television directed Hutus to slaughter Tutsis, whom they believed were preparing for their final victory. The radio announcer Georges Ruggiu (a Belgian immigrant with Hutu sympathies) urged his listeners that "graves were waiting to be filled."[66] In the carnage that followed, Hutus commit-ted genocide against Tutsis in Rwanda. All kinds of people—militiamen, soldiers, refugees recently arrived from Burundi, peasants, teachers, and doctors—killed roughly 800,000 people over the next four months, with guns, machetes, clubs, and even their bare hands.

Before casting off this violence as unthinkable, it's important to understand that—like the other violence we have learned about in this book—genocide in Rwanda was *entirely thinkable for the people who perpetrated it*. Remember that Hutus saw Tutsis as foreign invaders who had long tyrannized their homeland. Remember that many cited the Burundi genocide as proof that Tutsis aimed to exterminate Hutus. Remember that many had lived in refugee camps, where they shared stories about Tutsi horrors. Remember that the civil war had been already been raging for years, and the lines between civilians and soldiers often blurred. Remember that many also saw RPF victories as a prelude to the genocide of Hutus. With all that in mind, genocide does not become excusable, but it does start to become at least *thinkable*.

Most of the victims were Tutsis, though it could be hard to tell the difference between Hutus and Tutsis.[67] One survivor reported that some killers adopted a quick way to distinguish between the two, in cases of doubt. Stick a thumb into their nose. If it went in, release the person as a Hutu. If it didn't fit, kill the person as a Tutsi.[68] If this practice was used, it surely led to many misidentifica-tions. Hutus caught aiding Tutsis or even just refusing to kill them were them-selves killed. Hutu men in mixed marriages murdered their Tutsi wives to prove their loyalty. Some women killed as well or assisted in the killing. One teacher

---

65. Debate continues about who committed this attack. André Guichaoua, *From War to Genocide: Criminal Politics in Rwanda, 1990–1994*, trans. Don E. Webster (Madison: University of Wisconsin Press, 2015), 143–73.

66. Quoted in Oliver and Atmore, *Africa*, 345.

67. Much of the following draws on Mamdani, *When Victims Become Killers*, 222–47. Prunier, *The Rwanda Crisis*, 237–64.

68. Sommers, *Fear in Bongoland*, 32.

later confessed to killing children in his own classroom. A Lutheran minister explained, "Everyone had to participate. To prove that you weren't RPF, you had to walk around with a club. Being a pastor was not an excuse."[69]

The violence was not all-pervasive, however. Northern Rwanda saw little bloodshed. Some survivors later indicated that roughly 10 percent of Hutus protected Tutsis. Further, much of the violence seems to have been situational: a person who killed in one instance, helped a Tutsi escape in another. Here is not the place to investigate the patterns, but only to point out that even the most terrifyingly violent situations are more complex than the polarizing rhetoric used by extremists can explain.

The genocide in Rwanda sparked yet another massive refugee crisis. By July 1994, the RPF defeated the Rwandan army and established a new Tutsi-led government. Some two million Hutus fled Rwanda, some of whom had been perpetrators of genocide, but others merely feared retaliation. About half fled to Tanzania, but we will focus on the other half who moved into eastern Zaire, like those photographed in Figure 5.3, because of their role in promoting another set of conflicts. Their camps were a humanitarian disaster: tens of thousands died of disease and starvation. The UNHCR and the United States provided aid in the form of tents, food, water, and security forces. Some Hutu refugees—including former soldiers and Interahamwe militiamen—took tanks, armed vehicles, helicopters, and stockpiles of weapons and ammunition with them to militarized camps in eastern Zaire, which operated with tacit support from Mobutu Sese Seko and received military aid from France.[70] The camp at Lac Vert, for instance, served as a recruitment and training base for Hutu extremists to attack the new Rwandan government.

This massive refugee population exported the polarized Tutsi–Hutu divide into eastern Zaire. Hutu refugees from Rwanda formed alliances with Hutus living in eastern Zaire and attacked Zairian Tutsis, helping to radicalize people who previously had incentive to minimize differences between Kinyarwanda speakers. The influx of refugees also increased hostility among non-Kinyarwanda speakers in eastern Zaire against Hutus *and* Tutsis. Thus on April 28, 1995, a Zairian Parliamentary Commission demanded that all Kinyarwanda speakers "repatriate" to Rwanda and Burundi. Hunde, Nande, Nyanga, and others who described themselves as "indigenous" now treated Kinyarwanda speakers as a foreign threat, and even began forming armed militias of their own.

By 1996, eastern Zaire had become a militarized catastrophe. Out of the disorder, an anti-Mobutu coalition formed around Laurent Kabila, who launched the First Congo War (1996–1997). Internationally, Kabila had support from Rwanda, Uganda, and Angola, who each had strategic reasons to oppose Mobutu.[71] Within

---

69. Quoted in Mamdani, *When Victims Become Killers*, 226.

70. Keith Somerville, *Africa's Long Road since Independence: The Many Histories of a Continent* (London: Hurst & Company, 2015), 193–95.

FIGURE 5.3 Rwandan refugees in Zaire after the genocide.
Source: UNHCR

Zaire, Kabila also gained support from the Banyamulenge (a mixture of local and foreign Tutsis) as well as others who had grown tired of Mobutu's kleptocracy. Meanwhile, Mobutu's American allies sat out of the conflict, since the collapse of the Soviet Union had reduced their incentive to support his dictatorship as a bulwark against communism. In October and November, Kabila's allies burned Hutu refugee camps in eastern Zaire to the ground. Some Hutus fled back into Rwanda, but roughly 200,000 fled deeper into Zaire, spreading havoc as they went.

Kabila's forces toppled Mobutu's government in May 1997, returning the county's name to the Democratic Republic of the Congo (DRC). A year later, Kabila turned on his former allies, Rwanda and Uganda, and began providing training camps for Hutu extremists. Rwanda, insisting that Hutu refugees across its western border threatened its existence, expanded its attacks, occupying large sections of the eastern DRC. Kabila secured support from Angola, Namibia, Zimbabwe, Chad, and Sudan. The conflicts that followed, known as the Second Congo War (1998–2003) or Africa's World War, dwarfed all those previously discussed (and its aftershocks continue today). While the death toll is disputed, it was certainly over four times that of the Rwandan genocide of 1994, making it the bloodiest outcome of the Hutu–Tutsi refugee crises.[72]

71. Emizet F. Kisangani, "Conflict in the Democratic Republic of Congo," *International Journal on World Peace* 20, no. 3 (2003): 51–80.

72. Jason Stearns, *Dancing in the Glory of Monsters: The Collapse of the Congo and the Great War of Africa* (New York: PublicAffairs, 2012).

Conclusion

In all three of these cases, people took dramatic action to defend ideas about "Africa." However, in each case, colonial legacies—all brutal but each distinct— left different postcolonial inheritances that shaped what Africa meant. For Frantz Fanon and the FLN, Europeans were foreign oppressors who used racial differences to divide Africans. They urged people living on the African continent to see past the lines of race and religion that colonizers had used to divide them—and to fight in a shared African struggle for human dignity and self-actualization. Meanwhile, because of Uganda's racialized history under British rule, for Idi Amin, blackness became central to what it meant to be African, which led him to see Uganda's Asians as foreign oppressors. And in Africa's Great Lakes Region, people with the same dark skin and the same Kinyarwanda language understood themselves to be of mutually antagonistic races as a legacy of colonialism. Hutu perpetrators of genocide imagined Tutsis as a non-African race—an idea promoted by Europeans under colonial rule—that threatened their very existence. These three refugee crises do not offer a window into any shared African experience. Instead, these three histories provide a sense of the vibrant differences of people and places across the continent. It is only by appreciating the diverse legacies of colonialism that we can understand these different ideas about Africa, and the kinds of refugee crises that emerged in postcolonial Africa. I'm confident that if you explore other regions of Africa with further research, you'll see more of its great diversity, as well as troubling colonial legacies.

FURTHER READING

Allen, Tim, and Hubert Morsink, eds. *When Refugees Go Home: African Experiences*. Trenton, NJ: Africa World Press, 1994.

Arnold, Guy. *Africa: A Modern History: 1945–2015*. London: Atlantic Books, 2017.

Horne, Alistair. *A Savage War of Peace: Algeria, 1954–1962*. New York: New York Review Books, 2006.

Jamal, Vali. "Asians in Uganda, 1880–1972: Inequality and Expulsion." *Economic History Review* 29, no. 4 (1976): 602–16.

Lemarchand, René. *The Dynamics of Violence in Central Africa*. Philadelphia: University of Pennsylvania Press, 2009.

Malkki, Liisa H. *Purity and Exile: Violence, Memory and National Cosmology among Hutu Refugees in Tanzania*. Chicago: The University of Chicago Press, 1995.

CONCLUSION

This book argues that by placing refugee crises in historical and global perspective, we can reveal assumptions that humans have developed about what kinds of people deserve to live in what kinds of locations on this planet. Those worldviews took generations and sometimes even centuries to develop. In time, many people came to think about those metageographies as fundamental to political and social order. In the examples I have offered, people only resorted to violence and coercion because they viewed ideas that were historical—and thus *not* timeless—as essential to existence. This book emphasizes the role of the metageographies of continents and nation-states that have underlaid some of the most dramatic refugee crises in world history. Its premise has been that citizens today can develop more effective responses to refugee crises by studying world history. As such, I conclude by offering a brief model for doing your own research into refugee crises, based on what we have learned in the preceding chapters.

Let's start by picking a topic. According to the United Nations High Commissioner for Refugees, Syria is the origin of more refugees today than any other country—roughly 6,700,000 refugees since a civil war broke out there in 2011.[1] Let's start there. While over half fled to Turkey, let's focus on Lebanon instead, because it has the highest proportion of Syrian refugees per capita: they make up roughly 30 percent of its population. Now that we have a focus—Syrian refugees in Lebanon from 2011 to 2020—let's start to zoom in.

Civil war broke out in Syria in 2011, following massive antigovernment demonstrations that erupted across the Middle East. President Bashar al-Assad ordered a crackdown on civilian protestors that escalated into full-blown civil war between his secularist, nationalist government and a mix of rebel forces with diverse priorities. The conflict intensified after regional parties like Turkey and Iran began taking sides and offering support. In the summer of 2014, the Islamic State, an apocalyptic Sunni Muslim militant group that first emerged in Iraq, began launching attacks on Syrian territory in an effort to create a caliphate that could operate according to its version of Islamic principles and independent of Western interference. In response, the United States military—which had been waging a war in neighboring Iraq since its controversial invasion of 2003—began a bombing campaign in Syria as well. By the fall of 2014, the country was awash in violence.

About his time, mortars started hitting the house of a woman named Iman Rabieh. "We were just sitting there," Rabieh told an American reporter through a translator, "and then suddenly, a mortar just comes. You fear for your children. We were living in the middle of fighting in Syria, and we didn't leave. But then we were getting hit, and we didn't know from which direction it was even coming."[2] Rabieh, her husband, and children joined the roughly 1.5 million refugees who escaped to Lebanon. As she lamented, "I was a university student, and I never got to complete my education. I never got to graduate, and my whole future is lost just like that." In Lebanon, Rabieh and her family built a makeshift house in the Al-Salam refugee camp in Arsal, a town of about 10,000 people roughly 25 miles from the Syrian border.

Initially, Lebanon opened its borders to hundreds of thousands of refugees like Rabieh. Lebanon's government designated them as guests rather than as refugees, and thus made no formal legal commitment to protect their rights or guarantee them housing, education, and medical care. Still, in practice officials did what they could. But the small country could only offer a fraction of what was

---

1. These numbers can be found on that organization's website, https://www.unhcr.org/en-us/figures-at-a-glance.html.

2. Lama Al-Arian and Ruth Sherlock "Forced To Demolish Their Own Homes, Syrian Refugees In Lebanon Seek New Shelter," *National Public Radio*, June 22, 2019, https://www.npr.org/2019/06/22/733408450/forced-to-demolish-their-own-homes-syrian-refugees-in-lebanon-seek-new-shelter.

needed in the face of the humanitarian crisis. Refugees like Rabieh and her family began building housing for themselves in temporary, ad hoc settlements.

Meanwhile, back in Syria, the war dragged on. In 2016, Russia also began military operations in support of Assad's government, which had been an ally since the Cold War. Many observers worried that the conflict was becoming a proxy war between Russia and the United States. After peace negotiations failed, the war kept raging, and the refugees kept fleeing to Lebanon. By 2017, the Lebanese government instituted a $100 fee for Syrians wanting to migrate, which dramatically reduced inflows. In October 2019, the US President Donald Trump withdrew American troops from Syria, sparking near unanimous denunciations from Republican and Democratic lawmakers in his country, who claimed that it would allow Syria and Russia the upper hand against rebels. As of the time that I am writing these words, Assad's government controls most of the country. In the last rebel enclave, Idlib, Turkey and Russia reached a ceasefire to start March 15, 2020, just before the COVID-19 global pandemic hit the region.

Meanwhile, in Lebanon, the population gradually began to sour to the Syrian refugees. Lebanese accused them of increasing crime, promoting terrorism, and stealing their jobs. Locals verbally abused Syrians with racist taunts. The refugees felt isolated and marginalized. As a refugee named Mohammad explained in August 2016:

> In the beginning, we were welcomed and well-treated but for more than a year now we started to face harassment, restrictions on our movement ... Every time there is a security incident we are singled out as suspects. Even my children are being harassed by Lebanese students at school who blame Syrians for Lebanon's instability and rising criminality. My 16-year-old daughter asked me to leave Lebanon for a country that respects the human being but we have no choice except to stay here and put up with this situation.[3]

In February 2017, Fatima, a refugee from Aleppo, explained that even after four years in the Lebanese city of Nabatieh, her daughter was still not accepted by her classmates: "The first thing my daughter does when she comes home after school," Fatima explained, "is cry because her schoolmates keep telling her that she is a Syrian."[4] The situation is even worse for over one million undocumented

---

3. Samer Kadi and Oman Ibrahim, "Mounting Discrimination against Syrians," *The Arab Weekly*, August 7, 2016, p. 22.

4. Fatima's interview was conducted by researchers in 2017. Maha Yahya, Jean Kassir, Khalil el-Hariri, *Unheard Voices: What Syrian Refugees Need to Return Home*, Report published by the Carnegie Middle East Center, April 16, 2018, https://carnegie-mec.org/2018/04/16/unheard-voices-what-syrian-refugees-need-to-return-home-pub-76050. Her account can be found in the part of the report labeled "Policy Framework for Refugees in Lebanon and Jordan."

Syrians who lack residency permits. They face widespread exploitation by employers and evictions from landlords. Working illegally to support their families puts them at risk of arrest or expulsion back to war-torn Syria.

In recent years, the Lebanese government has taken steps to ensure that the refugees' stay is only temporary. Roughly 150 cities and towns have issued curfews for refugees. On April 10, 2017, the Lebanese army ordered the eviction of 10,000 Syrian refugees from their informal settlements. As a result, refugees have to move from the ad hoc communities they created, disassembling the very houses they built for themselves. "We have no idea where they are going to go now," Khaled Raad, a Syrian refugee in Arsal, told a reporter. "It's up to God now."[5] Iman Rabieh and her family are among the refugees forced to move from Arsal. "I am under so much pressure, I swear," she told a reporter in June 2019, "I can't breathe [since] yesterday, I've been under so much pressure . . . Anxiety, depression, it's an indescribable feeling . . . I have no idea where we will go."[6] Today, as COVID-19 begins to spread among the refugees, many do not seek medical treatment because they fear bringing attention to their undocumented status, which would surely bring deportation back to Syria.[7]

Lebanese who feel wary of the massive Syrian refugee population within their borders remember that their country has faced this problem before. In 1948, following the brief Arab–Israeli War described in chapter 4, Palestinian refugees flooded into Lebanon. Then, too, Lebanon opened its borders to asylum seekers. Then, too, the refugees and their hosts imagined the situation would be temporary. But as Israel consolidated its hold on the lands of former Mandatory Palestine, the refugees' stay became permanent. They were joined by another wave of Palestinian refugees fleeing Israel's victory in the 1967 Six-Day War. Many Palestinian refugees still live in Lebanon today. Some Lebanese associate them with political instabilities in their country, including the Lebanese Civil War (1975–1990), as well as Israeli bombing of pro-Palestinian militants operating in Lebanese territory. Without a plan for Syrians in Lebanon to return home, many Lebanese fear that history might repeat itself.

Syrian refugees feel abandoned not only by the Lebanese government, but also by the international community.[8] Many blame the United States and Russia,

---

5. "Destruction of Syrian Refugees' Shelters in Lebanon Condemned," *Aljazeera News*, July 5, 2019, https://www.aljazeera.com/news/2019/07/destruction-syrian-refugees-shelters-lebanon-condemned-190705102212768.html.

6. Al-Arian and Sherlock, "Forced To Demolish Their Own Homes."

7. Alice Fordam, "Syrian Refugees in Lebanon Fear Deportation for Seeking Coronavirus Test or Care," *National Public Radio*, April 6, 2020, https://www.npr.org/2020/04/06/825158835/syrian-refugees-fear-deportation-if-they-seek-coronavirus-testing-and-treatment.

8. Maha Yahya et al., *Unheard Voices*.

who intervened militarily in the conflict, but have taken no significant action to protect or defend its victims. Meanwhile, political discussions in the West have focused on how to keep refugees from coming to the West. Since January 2017, the United States government has banned Syrians from entering its borders. This decision violates the United States's commitment to the 1951 UN Refugee Convention, which treats refusing humanitarian aid to refugees as a violation of human rights. Some in the United States—including President Donald Trump— argue that their country cannot offer asylum to refugees because terrorists would take advantage of American generosity by sneaking in among the refugees and launching attacks. Some in Europe share these fears. However, in Europe there remains a deeper awareness in popular culture than in the United States of the tragedies of the two world wars—sparked by unchecked hypernationalism and racism—and of the injustices of colonialism. As a result, Germany has taken in over a million refugees since the start of the Syrian crisis, though not without significant controversy. Across Europe, governments are investing substantial resources to help refugees and their hosts learn to coexist. Meanwhile, a central goal of European diplomats has been too reduce the numbers of refugees arriving in their countries, by providing billions of euros in aid to Turkey and Lebanon to house refugees like Iman Rabieh and her family, who many Europeans fear might otherwise travel to Europe. Critics accuse European governments of outsourcing responsibility for humanitarian disasters.[9] Still, the European response has far exceeded any made by governments that have played an active role in the Syrian civil war, including Russia, Iran, and the United States.

What should our response be to the Syrian refugee crisis? Surely, if we are to make reasoned and mature decisions, we need to understand the nature of the conflict. But if we were to limit ourselves to internet searches of major news outlets, we might get the wrong impression that the causes of the crisis only go back to 2011 or are internal to Syria. We might be tempted to blame the refugee crisis on President Bashar al-Assad, whose willingness to ruthlessly crack down on antigovernment protestors drove Syria into war. Yet by studying other refugee crises in history, we now know that blaming any one leader for violence—from Ferdinand of Aragon in chapter 1 to Idi Amin in chapter 5—overestimates the individual agency of political elites, neglects the roles taken by ordinary people, and ignores the larger intellectual, political, and social frameworks that developed over time that shaped people's decisions. Questions of blame are necessary

---

9. "EU Policies Put Refugees at Risk," *Human Rights Watch*, November 23, 2016, https:// www.hrw.org/news/2016/11/23/eu-policies-put-refugees-risk.

for courts to assign punishments, for sure. But historical thinking forces us to see that individuals' decisions are always made only within specific contexts that took many years, and the involvement of many different people, to develop. This point does not absolve Assad or anyone else from responsibility for their actions. But it does assert that the causes of the crisis are more complex.

Another common way to misdiagnose refugee crises is to explain them as the outcome of the timeless character of a particular social group. For the Syrian refugee crisis, misinformed observers might cite something specific and unchanging about Islam, Arab culture, or the Middle East to explain the violence in Syria. But historical thinking shows us that such explanations are unpersuasive. They are rooted in myths of metageography that simplistically essentialize groups of people, and which only contribute to the same kind of fear-mongering rhetoric that has produced so many refugee crises. This response is part of the very problem it purports to diagnose.

A historical approach allows us to see beyond the limitations of both short-term thinking and timeless essentializing. Historical thinking allows us to see the long-term developments that have led to the emergence of worldviews, assumptions, and beliefs that help us understand more recent decisions—even ones we find abhorrent. It also allows us to see how various actors contributed to an outcome that was never inevitable, but could have unfolded differently had people made different decisions. At the same time, it avoids limiting our understanding of causality to questions of blame and guilt. Historical thinking also allows us to see how developments taking place far and near interacted, so that we never imagine that any set of outcomes took place in isolation of the rest of the world. In short, studying history helps us understand that the Syrian refugee crisis did not just pop up in 2011, nor was it the result of timeless or essential characteristics of any group of people. To understand its nature, then, we would have to understand it in the context of world history. But how do we do that?

In this book, I have offered a model for you to research a controversial and urgent issue facing the world—refugee crises—that seem to be at the heart of so much political debate today. I did not attempt to cover every refugee crisis in history but provided a series of case studies—organized chronologically and geographically—to explain the relationship between some of the big ideas shaping world history and the causes and outcomes of those crises. All along, it was my goal to provide you with some of the tools to use when considering controversies and questions facing the world, especially topics where the rhetoric is heated, the answers seems easy, and the sides appear neatly divided.

That's why I finished with the Syrian refugee crisis. As a historian, it's not my goal to tell you what to think or how to respond to this problem; it's my goal to help you make mature and reasoned decisions by guiding you toward historical thinking about that topic. After reading this book, I hope that you can think of some historical questions related to the Syrian refugee crisis that would help you make those decisions. Here are a few that you might start with, arranged roughly chronologically, following the chapters of this book:

- Where does the idea of "Syria" come from? What implications does it entail that might have shaped people's worldviews and actions? When and why was Syria first created as a political entity?
- What is the religious and ethnic makeup of the Syrian population? It has not always been that way (no feature of any human society has ever *always* been anything, after all!). So when did it emerge that way and why?
- Did nineteenth- and early twentieth-century European and American understandings of Syria or the Middle East shape life in Syria? If so, how?
- After World War I, did Syria become a mandate, like Palestine? If so, what long-term effects did colonialism have on Syrian politics, society, and identities?
- After World War I, did the contradiction between a world order based both on a principle of self-determination and the unwillingness of Europeans to abandon their colonies spark hostilities in Syria, as elsewhere in Asia?
- After World War II, did decolonization contribute to volatility in Syria, as elsewhere in Asia and Africa? If so, how?
- After World War II, did powerful, globally involved states like Britain, France, the Soviet Union, and the United States intervene in Syria, as they did elsewhere across the world? If so, how did those interventions shape politics, social relations, and identities in Syria?
- Between World War II and today, how have events going on in neighboring states—Iraq, Turkey, Israel, Jordan, and Lebanon—shaped politics, social relations, and identities in Syria?

Answering all these questions might take years, so it's a good idea to get an overview and then start specializing in one or two. The best place to start your reading would be recent histories of Syria and the Middle East aimed at non-specialists.[10] After you have some basic questions answered, you'll be in a better position to start reading more specialized literature that can answer one or more of these questions, or some of your own. As you read, you will also start to see debates among scholars and you'll have the opportunity to evaluate primary source evidence for yourself.

---

10. Something like these: James A. Reilly, *Fragile Nation, Shattered Land: The Modern History of Syria* (Boulder, CO: Lynne Rienner Publishers, 2019). Nicolas Pelham and Peter Mansfield, *A History of the Middle East*, 5th ed. (New York: Penguin Books, 2019).

To conclude, I'd encourage you to pull up a newspaper article or other media story online about another refugee crisis facing the world today. Go ahead. The book will be here when you get back. Got it? Good. Now, think about the kinds of questions I just posed about the history of the Syrian refugee crisis. Try developing a list of questions that the article you found does not have the time or space to answer. The point is not to criticize that particular journalist or that particular news source. Journalism simply plays a different role than history. The point is to start with what journalism does offer (an up-to-date and trustworthy account of the events going on now), and then to start learning more about how world history can help you understand that topic as well. Once you are better informed, you'll be in a position to see beyond today's heated political rhetoric and to make decisions about how to address the world that we have inherited.

INDEX

ABOUT THE COVER

The cover image is a photograph of a bronze statue, titled "Angels Unawares," that was unveiled at the Vatican on the 105th World Day of Migrants and Refugees on September 19, 2019. The artist, Timothy Scholz, depicted different refugees and migrants from world history. The title refers to a passage from the Christian New Testament (Hebrew 13:2) that reads, in the English Standard Version translation, "Do not neglect to show hospitality to strangers, for thereby some have entertained angels unawares." In December 2019, Jesse Spohnholz coincidentally passed by this statue just after finishing this book while he was visiting a friend in Rome. Photograph by author.